PENGUIN
SAFE COOKING FOR

Sylvia Hull was born in Newcastle-upon-Tyne and spent the early years of her life there. After graduating from Durham University she moved to London.

Growing up in an area with a tradition of good food, and having a mother in the hotel business, she always enjoyed cooking – inventively whenever possible. Her particular interest in feeding babies, however, began with her own two children. Both were fussy eaters, more interested in the sweet than the savoury, so she began to devise her own recipes.

Sylvia Hull was editor of the magazine *Mother & Baby* for ten years. To meet the requests for ideas and recipes which poured in constantly from desperate mothers she developed, with the help and advice of nutritional and medical experts, the recipes in her book *Cooking for a Baby* (1976), also published by Penguin. Realizing that parents today need more information about potential food hazards and how to avoid them, she has written this book.

Sylvia Hull is married to the cartoonist JON. They divide their time between a flat by the Thames at Richmond and a cottage in Wales, where they grow fruit, vegetables and herbs for the creative cooking they both enjoy.

SAFE COOKING FOR A HEALTHY BABY

SYLVIA HULL

ILLUSTRATED BY SUSAN HELLARD

PENGUIN BOOKS

PENGUIN BOOKS

Published by the Penguin Group
Penguin Books Ltd, 27 Wrights Lane, London w8 5TZ, England
Penguin Books USA Inc., 375 Hudson Street, New York, New York 10014, USA
Penguin Books Australia Ltd, Ringwood, Victoria, Australia
Penguin Books Canada Ltd, 10 Alcorn Avenue, Toronto, Ontario, Canada M4V 3B2
Penguin Books (NZ) Ltd, 182–190 Wairau Road, Auckland 10, New Zealand

Penguin Books Ltd, Registered Offices: Harmondsworth, Middlesex, England

Published in Penguin Books 1992
1 3 5 7 9 10 8 6 4 2

Filmset in $10\frac{1}{2}$/13 Plantin

Printed in England by Clays Ltd, St Ives plc

CONTENTS

CONTENTS

FOREWORD

Preparing food for a baby is one of the great responsibilities of parenthood. It encompasses the provision of enough food to satisfy the growing baby's appetite; the provision of a balanced diet to meet the baby's growing nutritional needs; the prevention of food-borne infections; and initiating a lifetime's attitude to eating and social behaviour.

In this straightforward text Sylvia Hull addresses these issues in a direct, clear and altogether sensible fashion. She defines the ideals, sets out the hazards, and offers an entirely practical approach to the preparation of a baby's meals. In this way the book will serve as a helpful companion to new parents and to all those looking for a healthy middle road through the warnings, rumours, food fads and nutritional exhortations that seem designed to confuse us in our shopping and preparation of every meal. We are guided from breast milk for the newly born through allowing the baby to signal his needs in the early weaning period to the essential nutritional advantage of a widely varied diet in early toddlerhood, all backed up with clear guidelines on food preparation and storage, the demystification of the use of freezers and microwaves and a rich set of recipes and menus for all occasions.

I hope you will form a partnership with this book and secure for your baby a safe, healthy and happy start on her or his lifetime's career of enjoying wholesome, nutritious and interesting meals.

David Baum
Professor of Child Health
Director, The Institute of Child Health
University of Bristol

INTRODUCTION

Most parents approach the introduction of solid food with a mixture of pleasurable anticipation – and apprehension. It is an exciting step forward, but today it is not just a question of when and what, but how to provide foods that are nutritious *and* free from potentially harmful substances.

Nagging uncertainties include how to avoid health hazards such as too much salt, sugar or fat. Then there are the risks of salmonella in eggs, BSE in beef, irradiation, additives, chemical residues and aluminium cooking utensils, among other recent scares. Every parent also wants mealtimes to be mutually satisfying – to be harmonious, and not fraught with anxious coaxing or food tantrums.

The purpose of this book is to enable you to achieve this. To help you select and prepare nutritious foods which are free from health hazards. To give you ample choice, with recipes to suit all feeding stages, tastes, pockets, time schedules and appetites. Many of the 'Quick Meals' take no longer than the opening of a can or a jar. I hope it will help you to establish a life-long pattern of safe and healthy eating, and a mealtime togetherness that is fun.

S. H.

ACKNOWLEDGEMENTS

My thanks to Tim Lang, Director of Parents for Safe Food, for kindly commenting on safety, health and hygiene aspects, and to Sally Parsonage, the nutritionist, for her excellent 'Feeding Guidelines', dietary advice and close vetting of all the recipes. I am also grateful to Dr Susan Jarrett for her willingness to cast an erudite eye over the whole manuscript, and to Professor Richard Lacey, the microbiologist, for specific advice on some of the more contentious food issues.

My special gratitude for invaluable feedback via their young offspring to Jenny and Martin Cross, Miriam and Peter Richardson, Barbara and Philip Shaw, and to Caroline Neale and her colleagues in the National Childbirth Trust who also, very generously, tried out some of the recipes.

AUTHOR'S NOTE

To avoid bias in the current anti-discriminatory climate, babies are sometimes assumed to be girls and sometimes boys, without any particular significance.

Choosing, Storing and Preparing Food for a Baby

This section is designed to help you plan your shopping, kitchen and food preparation for safety and good health. It will also make you aware of the hazards, and the avoiding action.

CHOOSING FOOD THAT IS HEALTHY AND SAFE

CHOOSING FISH

♦ Fish is a very healthy food for babies, children and adults. Once your baby is on to solid food, aim for at least two or three main meals of fish a week.

♦ Nutritionally, the cheaper fish, cod, haddock, whiting, coley and plaice, are every bit as good as the more expensive such as halibut, turbot, sole, mullet, brill, monkfish and wild salmon.

♦ Avoid fish such as herring, mackerel, sprats and sardines, in which the small fine bones are difficult to remove.

♦ Avoid smoked fish, too, such as kippers, bloaters, smoked cod, smoked haddock and smoked salmon. They are likely to contain nitrite and/or nitrate, both of which are preservatives banned in foods for babies and young children.

♦ When buying fresh, look for a good fishmonger. Fish should be:

◇ well-chilled, preferably on ice;

◇ fresh smelling, with no trace of ammonia;

◇ firm, with glistening skin and a bright colour;

◇ completely separate from any ready-to-eat products such as smoked salmon;

◇ served hygienically – look for hand-washing and clean finger nails;

◇ filleted, when necessary, in a separate, dedicated area.

♦ Once you have found a good fishmonger, take his/her advice on the kind of fish to buy, according to your preferences and purse.

♦ Frozen cod, haddock, plaice and other recommended white fish are healthy alternatives to fresh fish.

◆ Canned tuna and salmon are also nutritious and safe for babies.

CHOOSING MEAT AND POULTRY

◆ Although meat is high in protein and other nutrients, it is not necessary for a healthy diet. Other sources of protein (see our food chart on p. 54) are just as good.

◆ There has been uncertainty about the safety of eating beef, since it has been known that some beef cattle are infected with bovine spongiform encephalopathy (BSE), also dubbed mad cow disease. BSE comes from feeding contaminated sheep remains to cows – a practice now prohibited. While the Government has declared British beef safe, following measures taken to eradicate and prevent the spread of the disease, and eating infected beef has no immediate harmful effects, there is doubt about the longer term. It could be twenty years before we know for certain whether or not human beings can catch BSE from infected beef, as cattle probably did from infected sheep. Unlikely though this is, Professor Richard Lacey, a microbiologist, advises that beef should not be given to children. Others, such as Dr Helen Grant, a neuropathologist, argue that beef is safe as long as abattoirs' methods ensure no contamination of the meat by the spinal column or brain tissue. BSE is a disease of the nervous system. Most people agree that the risk is small, perhaps very, very small, but only you can decide for your family.

◆ If you eat meat and intend giving it to your baby, buy from a good butcher:

◇ Meat should be displayed in a refrigerated cabinet.

◇ Raw meat should be completely separate from cooked meats, with separate scales and sections in the display cabinets, and careful hand-washing between serving raw and cooked items.

◇ Sawdust should not be spread on the floor as it can contaminate the meat.

◇ The shop should be generally clean – a daily scrub out is a good sign.

♦ Choose lean meat that looks and smells fresh. It should be firm and free from any stickiness.

◇ Beef should be pink to red with creamy white brittle fat.

◇ Lamb should be bright red with brittle white flaky fat.

◇ Offal – liver, kidneys and heart – should look fresh and have no unpleasant odour.

◇ Chicken and turkey should have undamaged skin with no breaks, bruising or blood spots, smooth leg scales and firm white flesh. A yellow tinge, caused by feed, does not affect the eating quality.

◇ Ready-wrapped meat may hasten the growth of bacteria and prevent the recognition of meat that is 'off'. If you do buy it, look for the signs of freshness (above), check the sell-by date, and cook and eat accordingly.

♦ Best choices for babies:

◇ The freer rearing of sheep makes lamb, and more so mutton, and their liver and kidneys, the healthiest and safest choice in red meat and offal for young children.

◇ Chicken and turkey, particularly chicken, which is leaner, are healthy and safe, provided they are cooked properly (see 'Preparing and Cooking Food Safely', p. 38).

♦ Not recommended:

◇ Beef and cows' offal, because of the risk, albeit slight, of long-term health hazards associated with beef (see p. 4). Some recipes are, however, included for those who do choose to eat beef.

◇ Fatty meats such as pork, duck and goose, which are indigestible.

◇ Ready-minced meat, because it is usually very fat. Instead, buy some lean meat and ask your butcher to mince it for you or, better still, do it yourself if you have a mincer or chopper.

◇ Any ready-seasoned meat and poultry or made-up meat

products, like burgers, because of the added seasoning and the risk of contamination in the processing.

CHOOSING DAIRY FOODS
Milk

◆ Babies should continue to have breast milk or an approved formula milk up to at least the age of 6 months, when fresh pasteurized cows' milk may be introduced (see p. 17).

◆ Of all the fresh milks available in bottles and cartons, only pasteurized full-cream milks are recommended for children from 6 months to 2 years of age. After 2, semi-skimmed may be given, and after 5, skimmed, if the child is on a healthy mixed diet. The energy and vitamin content of semi-skimmed and skimmed milk are insufficient for a young child's needs.

◆ Milk should be stored in a refrigerated cabinet. Check sell-by dates before buying.

◆ Cows' milk occasionally causes allergies, such as asthma and eczema, in a small number of babies. Alternatives include:

◇ Pasteurized goats' milk, which is more expensive, has more saturated fats and lacks certain important vitamins and minerals. Discuss with your doctor or health visitor before changing.

◇ Soya milk, which is available as a substitute for breast or formula milk for babies under 6 months, and as an unflavoured soya milk drink for older babies. Again, it costs more.

◇ Other foods can replace milk – see those in Group B in 'Foods for a Balanced Diet', p. 54.

◆ Milks sold as follow-up milks for babies over 6 months are in no way better than breast, formula or fresh cows' milk.

Butter and margarine

◆ Butter is a pure, whole food with no adulteration, but unfortunately consists of 65 per cent saturated fat, too much of which can give rise to diseases later in life. So, buy a good quality butter, unsalted if possible, and use it sparingly in your baby's and your family's diet.

♦ Alternatively, use a good margarine. The best are the polyunsaturated margarines made from sunflower oil, which contain less saturated fat than butter.

♦ Low-fat spreads and other butter substitutes contain a high percentage of water.

Eggs

♦ Are eggs safe for babies? The answer is yes, as long as they are bought with care, stored and cooked properly. The salmonella bacteria has not been eradicated – infected eggs could come from almost any supplier. The advice from leading microbiologist Professor Richard Lacey – and repeated by the Government – is that eggs must be cooked until the white and yolk are solid, whether cooked individually or in baked or steamed dishes, in order to destroy any bacteria (see 'Preparing and Cooking Food Safely', p. 40, and recipes).

♦ What you should know and do when buying eggs:

◇ Shops should not keep them in a chilled cabinet or refrigerator (see 'Storing Food Safely', p. 32).

◇ Eggs claimed to be free-range, salmonella-free, imported, or from any other safe-sounding source, are not necessarily safer than battery-produced eggs.

◇ Check packing date and, if given, sell-by date. Use as soon as possible – within 4–5 weeks of the former date, a week of the latter.

◇ Open the carton, examine the eggs, and only buy if they are free from soiling by droppings, cracks or blemishes.

◇ Eggs should not have been washed, as washing exposes them to contamination through the shell.

Cheese

♦ Amongst hard cheeses, most of which contain some salt, a mild Cheddar is the most digestible for babies. Buy it unsalted if possible.

♦ Soft white cheeses are a healthy choice and an ideal instant food for babies (see recipes). If there is a choice, buy these cheeses in ready-packed cartons and not loose, by weight, to avoid possible contamination. Check use-by dates before buying and choose from:

◇ Cottage cheese – soft, lumpy texture, made from skimmed milk with added rennet and some salt.

◇ Curd cheese – smooth and firm. It is made from full-cream milk, allowed to turn naturally.

◇ Other healthy soft white cheeses include: quark, fromage frais – a staple part of many French babies' diets – Italian ricotta, Mascarpone and supermarkets' own-brand, pre-packed varieties.

◇ Choose only soft white cheeses made wholly from milk, without additives, if possible.

♦ Avoid creamy white cheeses enclosed by a crusty skin, such as Camembert and Brie, which have been known to become infected with listeria bacteria, through the rind.

♦ Other risky cheeses include those made from goats' milk and ewes' milk. Although many of these cheeses are perfectly safe, they are better avoided for the very young.

♦ Avoid processed cheeses or cheese spreads, most of which contain a high percentage of water, as well as undesirable additives.

Yoghurt

♦ Plain, natural yoghurt is healthy and safe for babies from about 4 to 6 months onwards.

♦ Those made from whole milk, rather than low-fat yoghurts, are healthier and taste less sharp.

♦ Strained Greek yoghurt is mild and creamier, higher in fat and more expensive – good for an occasional treat.

♦ Check use-by dates before buying.

♦ Avoid the flavoured varieties, as most contain sugar.

♦ Serve plain yoghurt as it is, or with your own additions, such as puréed fresh fruit (see recipes).

CHOOSING FRUIT

◆ Fruit is very healthy. Eaten fresh, there is no loss of nutrients, as there is in cooking. Include it as often as possible in your baby's, and the family's, diet – for breakfast, as a pudding or a between-meal snack. See 'Purées Galore', pp. 74–80, for fruits for the very young.

◆ When shopping:

◇ Choose sound fruits.

◇ Buy little and often so that it is eaten at its best.

◇ If it is available and you can afford it, buy organic produce to avoid any possible chemical contamination – it does cost more, but as more people buy it the price should come down.

Dried fruit

◆ Dried fruits are very nutritious, too, although they lack vitamin C and are sweeter than their fresh counterparts, because they have been left to ripen.

◆ To avoid a very sweet diet, therefore, do not serve them too often. Use occasionally with less sweet fruits and to sweeten puddings.

◆ Apricots, prunes and, occasionally, dates blend well into infant diets.

Frozen fruit

◆ These are excellent, though expensive, when certain fruits are out of season – blackcurrants, redcurrants, blackberries and raspberries are particularly good, and differ little from fresh fruit.

Canned fruit

◆ Fruit canned in natural fruit juice – not in sugary syrup – is a good stand-by for emergencies. As some of the nutrients are lost in the processing, it should not replace fresh fruit regularly.

CHOOSING VEGETABLES

♦ Like fruit, fresh vegetables are a very healthy choice. They contain valuable quantities of essential nutrients, a few of which are lost when cooked. They should be included in a baby's diet at least once a day, with some raw whenever possible.

♦ Tips for buying:

◇ Choose only fresh-looking produce.

◇ Green vegetables are particularly rich in essential vitamins, minerals and natural dietary fibre; the green pulses – peas and beans – are high in protein too.

◇ Potatoes are an important source of energy in the form of carbohydrate, vitamin C and some protein (for ways to serve see Potato plus, p. 211, and other recipes).

◇ Carrots, turnips, swedes and parsnips make nutritious and delicious puréed baby food.

◇ Serve vegetables raw to avoid any loss of nutrients from cooking as early as possible. Avocados can be given with first purées and others, such as tomatoes and sweet red peppers, shortly after about 6 months.

◇ If organic produce is available and within your budget, buy it to avoid the possibility of contamination by chemicals – the greater the demand, the sooner it will be more generally available, and cheaper.

Pulses

♦ These dried vegetables are a very healthy and inexpensive source of protein and other important nutrients. Some babies find them a little indigestible at first, but most accept them happily from 6 months or so.

♦ They include lentils, soya beans, haricot beans, aduki beans, mung beans, butter-beans, chick-peas, split yellow and green peas and whole green peas.

♦ All make soft purées, combine well with other foods and freeze well (see 'Meals to Freeze', p. 167–9, and recipes).

Canned vegetables

◆ Cans of certain vegetables, particularly tomatoes, sweet corn, baked beans and other pulses, are very useful stand-bys for speedy meal preparation (see 'Quick Meals', pp. 207–26).

◆ The effective heat treatment ensures they are safe, and only some of the nutrients are lost in the processing.

◆ Buy them without added sugar if possible, like Whole Earth's baked beans and other canned pulses, but avoid those with an artificial sweetener instead.

◆ Drain off any salty/sweet liquid and rinse pulses under the cold tap before using.

Frozen vegetables

◆ When fresh vegetables are in short supply, this is a healthy and safe way of enjoying some out of season. Particularly good are peas, runner or French beans, broad beans, broccoli, sweet corn and spinach, which is available in convenient packs of mini-sized portions.

CHOOSING RICE AND OTHER CEREALS

◆ *Rice* is a healthy food – nutritious, easy to digest, gluten-free and therefore not as likely to cause allergies as wheat and some other cereals. It is also inexpensive.

◇ Manufactured baby rice costs more and contains vitamins a baby on a normal diet does not need, but it can be useful in emergencies, and in cooking.

◇ Try ground rice or flaked rice (see 'Purées Galore', p. 84).

◇ Try the various rice grains: long-grain rice, risotto rice, or nutty-flavoured wholegrain brown rice, which is slightly more nutritious (see p. 84 and other recipes). Use pudding rice, too, which absorbs liquid well (see Baked rice and almonds, p. 154).

◆ *Maizemeal* or *cornmeal*, also gluten-free, is a yellow flour made from the nutritious whole grain, not to be confused with cornflour made from the starchy white centre. It makes a good custard/purée (p. 85).

◆ **Porridge oats** are a very nourishing and palatable traditional cereal.

◆ **Millet** is a nutritious cereal, rich in iron, which makes a porridge-like purée (p. 85), and combines well with fruits and vegetables.

◆ **Gram flour**, not strictly a cereal, is made from finely ground chick-peas. It makes a nutritious creamy 'custard' (p. 157), and can be used to replace egg in many recipes. Available from health food shops and Indian grocers.

◆ When buying all cereals and cereal products, avoid damaged or old-looking packets and check 'best before' dates, if relevant.

◆ For healthy, inexpensive, quick-to-prepare cereals see 'Choosing Convenience Foods', below.

CHOOSING CONVENIENCE FOODS

◆ The obvious advantages of convenience foods are often outweighed by the high sugar, salt and fat content, as well as additives. Chosen with care, many are healthy and safe for babies and young children.

Baby foods

◆ Manufactured baby foods are useful for emergencies. They are generally safe, barring deliberate contamination, though not as healthy as home-prepared food.

◆ Whether they come in cans, jars, or dried in packets to be reconstituted, look at the ingredients (see 'Check the Labels', pp. 20–24), and choose only natural foods that are free from added sugar, such as fruits, vegetables, rice or other cereals.

Canned foods

◆ Effective heat treatment renders canned foods safe, although there is some loss of vitamins and nutrients.

◆ Cans must be in good condition with no bad dents, rust or bulging outwards.

◆ Healthiest canned foods for a baby are:

  ◇ Baked beans, other pulses and sweet corn – preferably

with no added salt or sugar, but drain and rinse anyway – and Italian tomatoes (see also 'Choosing Vegetables', p. 10).

◊ Tuna and salmon, drained.

◊ Fruit canned in natural juice and not in syrup, for occasional use – there is some loss of nutrients in the processing.

Frozen foods

♦ Frozen foods are generally safe, and there is very little loss of essential nutrients in the processing.

♦ Safe and very healthy frozen foods for babies are:

◊ Frozen white fish such as cod, haddock, plaice, whiting, sole and coley, frozen in their natural state, with no coating such as breadcrumbs or batter, and no sauce.

◊ Frozen vegetables such as peas, broad beans, sweet corn and spinach.

◊ Frozen fruits such as raspberries, blackcurrants, blackberries and redcurrants.

♦ When buying:

◊ Select from the bottom of the cabinet if possible, where the temperature will be lower than near the top.

◊ Take frozen food home quickly, ideally in an insulated container, within an hour, and put it straight into your deep freeze or, if it is for more or less immediate use, your fridge.

Cereals

♦ Baby rice and other cereals commercially produced specifically for weaning are traditionally recommended. They do have the merit of being quick to prepare, but contain vitamins, which a baby on a normal diet does not need, and sometimes added sugar.

♦ For a quick cereal preparation, at much less cost, there are several alternatives:

◊ Ready Brek or a supermarket's similar own-brand instant oat cereal, which requires only the addition of hot milk.

◊ From a packet, an oatcake, a salt-free puffed rice cake, a Weetabix or a Shredded Wheat, crushed and softened with milk.

Pasta

♦ Pasta, being soft and easy to prepare, is ideal for babies – mash or liquidize at first.

♦ Choose from the smaller pastas such as rings and spirals, preferably wholemeal (see recipes).

Rusks

♦ All manufactured rusks contain a high proportion of sugar – some over a third. Even those claimed to be low in sugar can have as much as a sweet biscuit. So, for your baby's health, avoid bought rusks.

♦ It is easy to make your own – see p. 146.

♦ Alternatively, buy a packet of salt-free puffed rice cakes or Italian bread sticks and give your baby one to chew on.

Spreads

Some manufactured spreads conveniently double as healthy instant baby foods. They include:

Peanut and other nut butters

♦ These are very nutritious, but do have some added salt.

♦ Choose a smooth variety, not a crunchy one, to avoid choking on the nut bits, and preferably one with no added sugar, like Whole Earth's peanut butter. Cashew nut, hazelnut or Brazil nut butters are less widely available but can be found in health food shops. (See recipes in 'Quick Meals', pp. 207–26, and 'Finger Foods and Teatime Treats', pp. 149–50, for ways to use.)

Seed spreads

These are similarly nutritious and convenient:

♦ *Tahini*, made from creamed sesame seeds, has a distinctive, fairly strong flavour, so introduce it in very small quantities with, say, a puréed fruit or vegetable your baby enjoys. It can be used to replace eggs to bind baked dishes (see recipes), and a small quantity will thicken a thin purée.

♦ *Sunflower (seed) spread*, made from finely ground and creamed sunflower seeds – not to be confused with sunflower margarine – is similarly nutritious and easy to use, but milder in flavour and will not bind dishes.

Pure fruit spreads

♦ With no added sugar or artificial sweeteners, these are much healthier than traditional jams, which should be avoided. Once opened, they have to be refrigerated and eaten within 3 weeks.

♦ Whole Earth have a good range, available in health food shops. It is also easy to make your own, very healthy, fruit spread (see p. 150).

♦ Pure fruit spreads, amongst other naturally sweet products, provide healthy ways of flavouring plain yoghurt, of turning a cereal into a pudding, or sweetening a food that is unacceptably tart. Use in very small quantities – just enough to flavour or sweeten.

Honey

♦ This is 75 per cent sugar, and the nutrients it contains are negligible, but its occasional use is suggested for sweetening some recipes.

♦ Flavours vary according to the plants from which the bees have collected the nectar. Try to buy only those labelled 'pure' honey, if possible one from a named flower or a locally produced honey.

Fruit concentrates

♦ Fruit concentrates, available in bottles from health food shops, are made only from pure fruits such as apples, pears, apricots or blackcurrants. They are useful to sweeten tart fruits or flavour puddings, and for natural additive-free fruit drinks.

♦ They should be used in very small quantities as the concentration is 8 times normal strength.

♦ Although expensive initially, they go a long way and, once opened, will keep in the fridge for several weeks. Check 'best before' dates.

Soya products

♦ The highly nutritious soya bean is available in two convenient forms for babies – at health food shops and increasingly at supermarkets.

Tofu
- This is soft, custardy white cheese made from soya bean curd.
- It requires no cooking – an ideal instant baby food.
- It combines extremely well with most foods – hot or cold – and can be used in place of eggs in, say, a quiche (see recipes).
- Once opened, tofu will keep in the fridge for a few days, if covered with fresh water daily.

Soya flour
- This has been heat treated and requires no further cooking.
- A useful replacement for eggs in many recipes – one tea-spoonful provides instant added nourishment to fruit, vegetables, casseroles, bakes and other dishes (see recipes).

CHOOSING EXTRA VITAMINS?
- A baby's vitamin requirements are discussed in detail by nutritionist Sally Parsonage – 'Feeding Guidelines' pp. 49–50. In the UK, vitamin deficiency almost never occurs in babies and young children. The exceptions include premature and low birthweight babies and those not on dairy foods because of allergies, or because they are vegan, all of whom may require extra vitamins.
- The claims that additional vitamins improve a child's IQ have yet to be proven. Most experts remain sceptical.
- Too many vitamins could be harmful, so it is safer to resist pressure from persuasive product advertising that would have you believe otherwise.

Vitamin A and pregnant women or those likely to become pregnant
- Excesses of vitamin A, in particular, should be avoided by pregnant women or those likely to become pregnant.
- In October 1990 the British Government's Chief Medical

Officer advised these women not to eat liver or liver products, because some were found to contain exceptionally high levels of this vitamin. They also advised these women not to take dietary supplements containing vitamin A, over and above those prescribed as part of antenatal care.

◆ This advice followed birth defects in a small number of babies born to women abroad who had taken vitamin A supplements greatly in excess of the recommended dosage, and defects in a baby born to one woman in the UK who had consumed large quantities of liver every day.

◆ There is no positive evidence that excesses of vitamin A caused these defects, but while it is being investigated, the advice remains. Only women who are pregnant, or likely to become pregnant, are affected: other women, men, children and babies are not.

◆ Vitamin A is an essential nutrient and liver is not the only source: it can be obtained from carrots, margarine, dairy products, eggs, all green vegetables, tomatoes and other fruit.

◆ It is also recommended that women who stop eating liver increase their iron intake by eating more lean red meat and meat products, fortified breakfast cereals, bread and vegetables.

CHOOSING DRINKS
Milk
◆ When mixed feeding begins your baby should continue to have whatever milk he had before – breast or formula milk, both to drink and in cooking. Pasteurized full-cream cows' milk could be introduced from 6 months, but the latest Government Report on Infant Feeding (DHSS 1988) recommends the advantages of continuing breast milk or infant formula throughout the first year.

◆ Follow-up milks, commercially produced for the weaning stage, have no real advantage over the milks recommended above and are more expensive.

For a thirst
◆ If your baby is thirsty between meals the healthiest drink to offer is water – which should be boiled then cooled until he is about 8 months old – or well-diluted unsweetened fruit juice. Never add sugar to drinks for babies and young children.
◆ For safety of tap, filtered and softened water, see p. 41.

Fruit juice
◆ The healthiest fruit juice is freshly squeezed yourself. Alternatively, choose bottled, freshly squeezed juice, to be used within a day or two of purchase, or longer-life pure fruit or tomato juice, available in cartons and bottles. Make sure it is real juice only, with no added sugar or artificial sweetener, or other additives.
◆ Whichever fruit juice you use, always dilute one part juice with at least three or four parts water.
◆ Avoid fruit drinks such as those labelled 'drink', 'squash', 'crush', or 'ade' as in orangeade. They are mostly water, with sugar or artificial sweeteners, perhaps finely chopped pith and skin, artificial colouring and little, if any, real fruit juice.

Fruit concentrates
◆ Bottled fruit concentrates (see 'Convenience Foods', p. 15), can be used for real fruit drinks, too, but must be well-diluted, at least 8–10 parts water to one of the concentrate, and mixed well.

Baby fruit juices
◆ Many of the baby juices and drinks available contain added sugar – check the label.
◆ The healthiest are the pure, unsweetened baby fruit juices, which are just that, but they are expensive and have no real advantages. If used, they too should be well diluted with water.

Baby herbal teas
◆ Baby herbal teas should be avoided. They are largely sweetened water with a hint of herb.

Bottled water

◆ Normally there is no advantage in using bottled water. However, if the quality of tap water is in doubt, for instance, on holiday, it may be necessary.

◆ For safety, avoid any bottled water labelled 'natural mineral water'. It may include concentrations of nitrate or salt that a baby's immature kidneys cannot cope with.

◆ Bottled waters other than 'natural mineral water' are safe to use for mixing a baby's feed, as a drink, or in cooking. Like tap water, bottled water should be boiled before use up to the age of about 8 months.

CHOOSING NUTS

◆ Whole or cracked nuts, or nut bits, should NOT be given to young children until they are about 5, as they could cause choking.

◆ Nutritious and safe when ground powder fine, nuts are a very useful ingredient in dishes for babies aged about 6 months upwards. They combine well with foods like fruit, vegetables, yoghurt and rice (see recipes).

◆ With the exception of walnuts, which can be bitter, nuts such as almonds, hazelnuts, cashews, Brazil nuts or peanuts (unsalted of course), as well as the less familiar pine nuts, are safe and healthy for babies.

◆ Almonds are available everywhere, conveniently ready-ground (intended for paste for cakes). Other nuts are sometimes available finely ground, particularly in health food shops. Otherwise they can be ground with a blender or chopper designed to do this.

◆ Buy whole nuts ready-shelled and packaged – unless you prefer to shell them yourself. Choose undamaged packs and check 'best before' dates.

◆ There was a scare over a mould on peanuts, aflatoxin, a few years ago, but this has now virtually been eliminated with careful screening and sorting.

♦ Smooth peanut butter and other nut butters are a convenient way of serving nuts to babies.

CHOOSING SEEDS

♦ *Sunflower seeds,* like nuts, should never be given whole to a young child, as they could cause choking. However, they are very nutritious – rich in protein, minerals and vitamins – and, ground powder fine, they combine well with many foods (see recipes). Available from health food shops, choose undamaged packs and check the 'best before' date.

♦ *Sunflower (seed) spread,* not to be confused with sunflower margarine, is made from ground sunflower seeds and is convenient to use. Available from health food shops.

♦ *Sesame seeds* are similarly nutritious. They do not easily grind powder fine, but are good in dishes such as savoury bakes, or later, when your baby is experimenting with textures, combined with a favourite fruit or vegetable (see 'Quick Meals', pp. 207–226).

♦ *Tahini* is a spread made from creamed sesame seeds, available from health food shops. It is smooth and has no added salt, but because of its distinctive flavour is best introduced in small quantities with other foods (see also 'Choosing Convenience Foods – Spreads', p. 14).

CHOOSING COOKING OIL

♦ The healthiest cooking oils are high in unsaturated fats and polyunsaturates and low in saturated fats. They include sunflower, soya, corn, sesame and olive oil.

♦ Oils to avoid are those that are high in saturates and any labelled 'vegetable oil', which could include such oils.

CHECK THE LABELS

Information on labels can help you choose healthy foods. It can also confuse. Here are a few guidelines.

♦ All foods must be named or described on labels and pre-packed foods must give ingredients, too.

♦ Ingredients are listed according to their weight, the heaviest first. So if, for instance, water comes first in a baby food contents list, it contains more of that than anything else. Choose instead one with say a fruit, vegetable or cereal first, with few, if any, other ingredients.

Sugar

♦ Sugar should be avoided as far as possible in foods for babies (see pp. 27–8).

♦ So that those who do not want a very sweet product are not discouraged, manufacturers might include sugar under several

different names, whereas if they were combined under one name, it would be at or near the top of the list. So, watch for and avoid, if possible, any one or more of these terms for sugar: sucrose, glucose, dextrose, fructose, honey, lactose, treacle, molasses, invert sugar, corn syrup – or any other syrup. Sorbitol, mannitol and xylitol are non-sugar sweeteners, also to be avoided.

◆ 'Low sugar' and 'no added sugar' are not reliable guides. The product could still be very sweet and, even under the latter claim, contain sugar in one or other of the forms referred to above.

◆ Some product labels to check for unnecessary sugar are: baby foods and drinks; cans of beans (drain off any sweet liquid and rinse beans); nut butters; fruit drinks and juices; baby medicines, including gripe waters. (All gripe waters also contain 5 per cent of alcohol – more than many beers and lagers – a potentially harmful amount for a small body.)

Additives

◆ By law, all additives must be listed in the ingredients, including those prefixed with E, which are regulated by the European Economic Community (EEC).

◆ They have no health value, with the exception of preservatives which may keep food safer, and their long-term effects are not yet known.

◆ Of nearly 4,000 additives in use in the UK, 3,500 are flavour enhancers!

◆ Most additives are prohibited in baby foods, which must not, by law, contain artificial sweeteners, flavour enhancers, certain preservatives and colouring agents, with three exceptions which are also essential vitamins: Riboflavin (E101), an orange yellow; Riboflavin (E101a), a yellow derivative of this; and Carotene (E160a), which could be yellow, orange or red.

◆ The general rule should be to keep additive intake to a minimum, as far as possible. They are not part of the ordinary ingredients. Good, wholesome food should be the aim.

Fats and oils

◆ Too much fat in a young child's diet is neither safe nor healthy, but some fat is necessary, and the quality varies.

◆ Healthy fats are polyunsaturates, as in sunflower oil, for instance, so the higher the proportion of these in the total fats on the label, the better (see also 'Choosing Cooking Oil', p. 20).

◆ Saturated fats, which include hydrogenated oils, are unhealthy. They can cause raised blood cholesterol and possibly heart disease and other disabling conditions later in life. They should, therefore, form only a small percentage of the total fats listed on the label.

Irradiated food

◆ Food irradiation is now permitted in the UK provided that foods, or certain ingredients so treated, carry a declaration specifying that they have been 'irradiated' or 'treated with ionizing radiation' – so check the label.

◆ By allowing its introduction, the Government considers it is safe, but consumer groups, the British Medical Association and most food retailers and growers have reservations.

◆ The method works by subjecting food to ionizing radiation which kills all living organisms, including harmful bacteria and moulds. This reduces the risk of food poisoning and extends the shelf-life.

◆ Foods likely to be irradiated include poultry, prawns, shrimps, dried herbs and certain fruits and vegetables.

◆ Although irradiated food looks fresh, the process results in a loss of vitamins, and there are doubts about aspects of its safety. For instance:

◇ There is uncertainty about whether or not the process destroys all the harmful substances – toxins from the destroyed bacteria may remain.

◇ It is difficult to ensure that every item of food has been adequately treated, and there is no means of checking.

◇ Contamination may occur after irradiation if packaging is flimsy.

◇ Little, if anything, is known about the long-term medical consequences of eating irradiated food.

◇ There are no plans to check these and other potentially hazardous aspects.

♦ Some big consumer outlets share the doubts about irradiation and will not stock irradiated foods.

♦ Whatever your decision for the family, it is probably advisable not to give irradiated foods to your baby, given the vulnerability of the very young.

'Best before' and 'use by' dates

♦ Most foodstuffs carry a 'best before' date which indicates how long the food continues to be at its best, e.g. crisp biscuits may become soft.

♦ Highly perishable foods such as milk or meat products, which could become a safety risk, carry a 'use by' date. It is an offence for food to be sold beyond a 'use by' date.

FOODS TO AVOID OR OFFER CAUTIOUSLY

Additive-containing foods – avoid whenever possible

♦ Additives have no nutritional value and may be allergy-causing and carry other health risks for babies and young children. Their long-term effects are not yet known (see 'Additives', p. 22).

Allergy-causing foods – offer cautiously

♦ Certain foods cause allergic reactions such as asthma, eczema, skin rashes and hyperactivity, in a few children.

♦ Offer such foods with particular caution, especially if you have an allergy problem in your immediate family, and watch for any reaction.

♦ Suspect foods include:

◇ wheatflour in bread, cakes, sauces etc.

◇ fresh cows' milk

◇ egg white (offer at about 8 months)

◇ nuts

◇ oranges and other citrus fruits

◇ goats' milk

♦ Food additives such as colourings and antioxidants can give rise to allergic reactions too, but they should not be given to babies and young children anyway (see 'Additives', p. 22).

Beef – probably avoid

♦ Some beef cattle are infected with bovine spongiform encephalopathy (BSE), also known as mad cow disease. Although there are no immediate harmful effects from eating infected beef, and the Government has cleared it as safe, the long-term implications are uncertain (see 'Choosing Meat', pp. 4–6).

Chillies and other strong flavours – avoid for the very young

♦ Babies enjoy bland foods and, until their palates develop, most will not be able to accept very hot, spicy and other strongly flavoured food.

Cook chill foods – avoid

♦ Ready-cooked dishes, such as portions of chicken, sold from chilled cabinets in shops, should not be given to babies and young children. The risk of harmful bacteria being present in these foods is too great for the very young.

Cream – avoid for the very young

♦ The high fat content of cream is too rich and indigestible for most babies.

Eggs – take precautions

♦ Eggs are very nutritious and, with precautions, safe for babies. See 'What you should know and do when buying eggs', p. 7, 'Storing Food Safely', p. 32 and 'Preparing and Cooking Food Safely', p. 40. For safe cooking methods, see recipes.

Ewes' milk – avoid

♦ Ewes' milk is not recommended as a regular milk for babies.
♦ If it is given as part of a varied diet for older children it should be pasteurized or, if not, boiled.

Fat – avoid saturated fats and any excesses

♦ Avoid fatty foods such as crisps and other bag snacks, and fatty meats such as duck, goose and pork (see also 'Check the Labels', p. 23).

Fried foods – avoid

♦ As the coating of fat on fried food has to be digested slowly, before the food itself, it puts a great strain on an immature digestive system.

Garlic – with caution

♦ Like onions, the flavour of garlic is too strong for the bland palates of most young babies. Some, however, take to it happily from an early age. If you enjoy garlic yourself and want to try, begin with a hint only, from 6 to 8 months of age.

Goats' milk – with caution

♦ Goats' milk is sometimes recommended for babies over 6 months who are unable to tolerate cows' milk. It must be pasteurized.

♦ As it is deficient in certain essential nutrients, extra minerals and vitamins are needed to compensate. A doctor or health visitor would advise.

Ham and other cured meats – avoid

♦ Cured meats are likely to contain nitrite and nitrate, preservatives that are banned in foods for babies and young children.

Irradiated food – avoid

♦ See pros and cons in 'Check the Labels', pp. 23–4.

Manufactured fruit drinks – avoid most

♦ For health hazards associated with commercially produced fruit drinks and juices, see 'Choosing Drinks', pp. 17–19.

Marmite – avoid

♦ Contrary to conventional wisdom and the manufacturer's continuing insistence, Marmite is not a healthy food for babies and should be avoided. It is about 10 per cent pure salt and the most recent Government Report on Infant Feeding (DHSS 1988) says that salt should not be added to a baby's food.

Onions – with caution

♦ For many babies the taste of onion is too strong, although some will devour onion-flavoured foods eagerly. It is probably safest to wait until your baby is about 8 months old and introduce it into his food gradually.

Rhubarb – avoid

♦ The acidity of this fruit can easily upset a very young digestive system, so it is safer not to introduce it until your child is into his second year.

Rusks from a packet – avoid

♦ All manufactured rusks contain a high proportion of sugar (see 'Choosing Convenience Foods – Rusks', p. 14).

Salt – avoid

♦ Salt should not be added to food for babies until they are over a year old – and then just an occasional dash, if at all.

♦ A baby's requirement is already met by the salt/sodium present in foods like milk, cereals and bread.

♦ A baby's immature kidneys are unable to deal with too much salt. An excess of salt could also be a contributory factor in causing hypertension and, in turn, heart disease, later in life.

♦ Salty foods such as crisps, other bag snacks and Marmite (referred to above), should also be avoided.

Semi-skimmed or skimmed milk – avoid

♦ See 'Choosing Dairy Foods – Milk', p. 6.

Smoked fish – avoid

♦ See 'Choosing Fish', p. 3.

Soft creamy cheeses in a rind – avoid

♦ See 'Choosing Dairy Foods – Cheese', p. 8.

Strawberries – avoid

♦ Acidity and indigestible seeds render these delicious fruits unsafe for babies. Wait until the second year to introduce them cautiously.

Sugar – avoid as far as possible

♦ Sugar should not be added to a baby's food. It causes tooth decay, as well as obesity, which increases the risk of life-threatening diseases later in life.

♦ If sweetening is needed, use a naturally sweet fruit, such as pear, banana, apricot or date (see Date purée, p. 76), a very small quantity of a fruit concentrate or, occasionally, a little honey.

♦ For ways of avoiding hidden sugar in manufactured foods, see 'Check the Labels – Sugar', p. 21.

Sweet drinks in a dinky feeder – avoid

♦ No sweet drink, including naturally sweet fruit juice, should ever be given to a child in a dinky feeder. The slow flow from the teat bathes the gums in sugary, and perhaps acid, liquid, thus creating the most favourable conditions for tooth decay.

Unpasteurized milk – avoid

♦ Without the effective heat treatment involved in pasteurization, milk could spread infections such as salmonella and tuberculosis.

Whole nuts – avoid

♦ Because of the danger of choking on them, whole nuts and nut bits should not be given to babies – or young children – until they are about 5 years old.

STORING FOOD SAFELY

IN THE REFRIGERATOR

The low temperature of refrigeration keeps food safely by preventing the growth of food-poisoning bacteria. It does this only for a limited time and the bacteria already present in the food are neither reduced nor destroyed.

Tips for safety

◆ Do not overload. Tightly packed food prevents the circulation of cold air.

◆ Store different types of food, particularly raw and cooked, separately, preferably on different shelves, the lower ones for raw food, to prevent it contaminating the rest.

◆ Wrap each of the stored items individually to prevent cross-contamination. Leafy vegetables and salad ingredients should go unwashed, in plastic bags, in the crisper compartment. Any leaves should be removed from root vegetables before wrapping and storing them.

◆ Cool warm food before refrigerating. Do it quickly – within an hour and a half, for safety. Stand in iced water if necessary.

◆ Stick to approximate safe storage times.

Raw food:
◇ meat (to be cooked thoroughly)   3–5 days
◇ fish   12 hours
◇ vegetables and salad ingredients   1–5 days

Cooked food – cool quickly first:
◇ meat, poultry, stews and casseroles   2 days
◇ opened cans, including baby food (transfer to a clean container and cover)   24 hours
◇ jars, including baby food (cover with lid or plate) 24 hours

⬦ baby food, if freshly cooked, cooled quickly
and covered   24 hours
⬦ left-over vegetables   avoid
⬦ cooked pulses   2–3 days
⬦ left-over gravies, sauces, custards   never

Dairy produce:

⬦ milk and cream: unopened   2–3 days
⬦ milk and cream: opened   2 days
⬦ cheeses: * unopened   according to
'use by' dates or
for as long as the
appearance is fresh
and acceptable
⬦ cheeses:* opened   up to 5 days
⬦ packeted products like butter and   according to
margarine *   'best before' dates
⬦ eggs   never (see p. 32)

◆ Keep the fridge temperature between 0 to 5 °C. A fridge
thermometer that reads from − 5 to + 10 °C is helpful, placed
where it can be seen easily. Check after the door has been
closed for some time, say overnight. Alter fridge setting, if
necessary, to make sure the temperature is below 5 °C.

◆ To maintain a safe temperature:
⬦ Don't place your fridge next to the cooker.
⬦ Don't open the door for longer than necessary.
⬦ Keep the back housing dusted.

◆ Defrost and clean your fridge regularly. Unless it does it
automatically, defrost once a week. Clean weekly, preferably
when it is nearly empty, before your big shopping day. Use
warm water with bicarbonate of soda and dry well.

---

* To allow flavour and softness to return to hard cheese, butter and
margarine, it could be removed from the fridge an hour before use.

USING A FREEZER TO FULL ADVANTAGE

◆ Having a freezer should make cooking for your baby easier and more enjoyable. It is worth taking a little trouble to organize it for safety and convenience (see 'Meals to Freeze', p. 166).

◆ Chest freezers are preferable to uprights, if you have a choice. Otherwise, shelves with sides minimize heat entry.

◆ The temperature should be –18 °C (or under) to – 23 °C (0 to 10 °F). Buy a freezer thermometer to ensure this.

◆ Open the door as little as possible, and not at all if there is a power cut.

◆ When buying frozen foods, get them home and into the freezer quickly, ideally within an hour, and use an insulated container to carry them, if possible, to prevent defrosting.

◆ Pack all items in sealed freezer bags or lidded containers to prevent cross-contamination.

◆ Label each with the name of the food and the date.

◆ Keep raw meat and fish apart from foods like ice-cream, puddings and cakes that will not be cooked, to prevent cross-contamination.

◆ Organize contents with those to be used first, like baby foods, for instance, in the most accessible place.

◆ Keep a notebook listing what you have frozen and when and delete items when used.

◆ Finally, to keep your freezer in safe working order, defrost and clean every 3 months, when it is as empty as possible. Keep remaining food cold – in the fridge, in insulated boxes, or wrapped in plenty of newspaper or old blankets. Remove any spilled food and clean with warm water and bicarbonate of soda.

IN CUPBOARDS

◆ In place of cool larders, most kitchens now have room-temperature cupboards and shelves where many foods can be stored safely, provided they are dry and looked after routinely.

Cupboard care

♦ Arrange all perishable items according to 'best before' and 'use by' dates, with those to be used first at the front.

♦ All food cupboards and shelves should be turned out and cleaned at least once a month, when any items past their fresh dates should be discarded.

♦ Spillages should be wiped up immediately.

♦ Any sign of infestation – droppings or gnawed packets – should be acted on straight away. Take expert advice; if necessary, the Environmental Health Department of your local authority will help.

Safe for which foods?

Eggs

♦ These should be kept at room temperature and not in the fridge because:

◇ The protective covering over the tiny pores in the shell could be destroyed by the condensation in a fridge.

◇ The centre of a refrigerated egg may not reach a high enough temperature during cooking to kill any salmonella bacteria.

◇ During transportation from farm to packing station to shop – 10–15 days – the eggs will have been stored at room temperature anyway.

♦ Ideally, eggs should be stored for no longer than 4–5 weeks after the packing date, a week after the 'sell by' date.

Dry foods

♦ Unopened foods such as rice, lentils, pulses, flour, baby milk powder, cereals, nuts and pasta, are safe at room temperature, but use by any 'best before' dates and keep dry.

♦ Bacteria flourish in moisture. Once opened, transfer to airtight containers to protect from dampness and pests.

Canned food (including baby food)

♦ This is safe at room temperature until opened – cans should be sound with no bad dents, bulging or sign of rust.

♦ All cans in supermarkets should now carry 'best before'

dates. Any that don't should be marked with date purchased and used within two years for safety.

♦ Once opened, transfer any left-over contents to a clean lidded container and refrigerate for up to 24 hours.

Food in jars (*including baby food*)

♦ This is also safe at room temperature until opened. Any left in the jar can be covered and refrigerated for up to 24 hours.

♦ Spreads such as peanut butter and tahini, in screw-top jars, are safe at room temperature, but should be used by 'best before' dates.

♦ Jars of pure fruit sugar-free spreads are safe, but once opened should be kept in the fridge and used within 3 weeks.

Root vegetables

◆ These are safest in the fridge, if space permits, otherwise in a cool dark place.

Concentrated pure fruit juice and pure fruit concentrates

◆ These come in cartons and bottles and are safe at room temperature if unopened and within their 'best before' dates.

◆ Once opened, they should be kept in the fridge and used within the time specified on the package.

CLING FILM

◆ Useful though it is for protecting food from contamination, cling film, even when labelled 'non-PVC' or 'plasticizer-free', should not be allowed to come in contact with food. There is a debate about whether potentially harmful substances in the cling film may migrate into certain foods, particularly fatty ones like cheese, butter and cakes. Although it could still be used to cover food in a container, provided it is well away from any contact with the food, play safe – if you store food in a bowl in the fridge, cover with a plate.

HYGIENE

IN THE KITCHEN
Babies are particularly vulnerable to infection, so hygiene in preparing and cooking food takes on a new importance.

Points to watch

◆ The ideal safe temperature for a kitchen is the lowest that is comfortable.

◆ Keep the preparation of raw food – meat, poultry, fish and vegetables – quite separate from the preparation of food that is not going to be cooked, to reduce the risk of contamination.

◆ Hand towels, tea towels and dish cloths should be changed daily, if possible. They can be a source for spreading infection.

◆ It is more hygienic to allow dishes to drain dry, or to use disposable kitchen towels, than risk contamination from a tea towel.

◆ Rubbish bins should be kept firmly covered, away from food, and disinfected regularly.

◆ All surfaces and equipment should be washed with hot water and a detergent between using for different foods, removing all food debris and dirt. Dry them, too, preferably with disposable kitchen towels.

◆ Flies should be kept away, with a safely placed deterrent, if necessary. Use aerosol sprays warily and never near food.

◆ Any foods left in the open should be covered to prevent contamination from stray insects.

◆ If you have a pet:
  ◇ Keep it away from your food, the working surfaces and cooking utensils to avoid transmitting diseases that cats, dogs and other pets can pass on to young children.

◇ Don't allow it to lick your baby, particularly her face or fingers, for the same reason.

◇ Store pet food in a tightly covered box in the fridge or a separate part of the kitchen.

◇ Provide separate feeding bowls and utensils and keep these apart from the family's.

◇ Remove any excreta immediately.

YOU AND YOUR BABY

◆ Always wash your hands before preparing and serving your baby's food, as well as after touching dirty nappies, pets, the rubbish bin, or going to the toilet.

◆ Once your baby is touching food, wash her hands, too, before and after meals.

◆ Provide your baby with a clean bib or paper napkin at every meal and remove immediately afterwards.

◆ Left-over food from your baby's dish should be thrown away, in case it has become contaminated with bacteria.

◆ Until your baby is about 7 months old, it is advisable to sterilize her dishes, spoons and cups by immersing in Milton or a similar solution or, for metal items, boiling them.

FOOD POISONING

◆ Food poisoning can be mild or severe.

◆ The symptoms – stomach pain, vomiting and/or diarrhoea – may appear within an hour or as long as 5 days later.

◆ Your doctor should be consulted if symptoms are painful or persistent.

◆ If you suspect a particular food, keep a sample of it for your doctor in a sealed container.

◆ The very young are particularly vulnerable and need special protection. To minimize the risk for your baby:

   ◇ Try not to prepare food for him if you are suffering from vomiting or diarrhoea.

   ◇ Follow all recommendations made in this section.

   ◇ In particular, cook high risk foods, such as poultry, meat and eggs, really thoroughly, and wash any fruit or vegetable to be served raw especially well.

PREPARING AND COOKING FOOD SAFELY

There are plenty of specific recipes further on in the book. Here are the basics of safe and healthy baby food preparation, with some additional cautions on risky foods and utensils. While foods can be more palatable hot, there is no reason why many foods should not be served cold, as long as your baby accepts it, and it is thoroughly cooked, if appropriate. It is every bit as nutritious, if not more so, because some nutrients could be lost in the heating.

Fish
◆ Fish preparation, and any utensils used, should be kept separate from other foods.
◆ If fresh, fish should be washed and dried with kitchen paper before it is cooked.
◆ Frozen fish can be cooked safely without thawing first, but 5–10 minutes additional cooking time should be allowed.
◆ Healthy ways of cooking include: poaching, steaming, baking, grilling, and simmering below boiling point. Avoid frying.
◆ When flakes separate easily, fish is cooked.
◆ Always check carefully for stray bones before serving.

Meat and poultry
◆ The preparation of raw meat and poultry, and utensils used, should be kept apart from cooked food and vegetables, in case of cross-contamination.
◆ Fat and skin should be trimmed off beef, lamb, mutton and poultry pieces, before cooking, as any excess of fat is unhealthy.

♦ Poultry should not be stuffed as it prevents hot air circulating. Cook any stuffing separately.

♦ When frozen:

◇ Completely thaw meat and poultry before cooking – remove freezer wrapping, place in a dish deep enough to contain the juices, cover, and put in the bottom of the fridge, or in a cool room, 15 °C (60 °F).

◇ For a small piece of chicken allow about 1 day in the fridge or 12 hours in a cool room; double this for a small to medium-sized chicken. Remove giblets as soon as they are sufficiently thawed.

◇ A warm room will hasten thawing, but also encourage the growth of bacteria.

◇ A microwave oven should not be used for defrosting meat or poultry for a baby. Uneven heat could warm one part unsafely, before the rest has thawed.

♦ Healthy ways of cooking meat and poultry for babies include: poaching, steaming, grilling (with little or no fat), baking, casseroling, boiling, and slow roasting (with 1–2 tablespoons water, little or no added fat and covered with a lid). Drain off surplus fat after grilling and roasting, or cool with juices and skim as in 'Small Stocks', p. 111. Avoid frying, which is too fatty and indigestible.

♦ Joints of meat and poultry must be cooked right through to ensure that any harmful bacteria are destroyed. A meat thermometer is useful to check the temperature, which should reach at least 70–80 °C (160–180 °F), in the centre for 2 minutes. Or pierce with a skewer (between leg and breast in a bird) – it is cooked when juices run clear, with no sign of blood.

Milk for cooking

♦ For cooking, use whatever milk your baby has been having – breast or a formula milk – until he is at least 6 months old.

♦ Whole pasteurized cows' milk may be introduced after 6 months, but there are health advantages in continuing breast milk or infant formula throughout the first year (see also p. 17).

Eggs

◆ For babies and young children, eggs should be cooked until the white and yolk are solid. This is official Government advice, following the outbreaks of salmonella food poisoning associated with eggs.

◆ Safe methods include boiling, scrambling, baking or steaming, as long as the egg is well cooked and firm and dry (see 'Ways with Eggs', pp. 116–19, and other egg recipes).

◆ Well-cooked egg yolks may be given to babies from the age of 6 months (see Egg yolk purée, p. 86).

◆ Egg whites should not be offered with the yolk until about 8 months, in case of digestive or allergic reactions.

◆ Raw egg and lightly cooked egg should never be given to babies.

◆ As with all cooked foods, egg dishes should be eaten as soon as possible after cooking. If they are not to be eaten immediately, cool quickly and refrigerate for up to 12 hours.

Fruit and vegetables

◆ Wash all fruit and vegetables very thoroughly, even if they are organically grown. Use a vegetable brush if appropriate and peel, too, to remove any chemicals or bacteria on the skin.

◆ With potatoes, scrub well, boil or steam and peel when cooked, to avoid loss of nutrients from just under the skin.

◆ To minimize the loss of vitamin C and preserve other nutrients, colour and flavour, steam vegetables and fruit, or put into about ½–1 inch of boiling water and simmer until just tender. Drain and use cooking liquid if possible in soup, to soften purées, or as a drink.

◆ Serve vegetables as soon as you can after they finish cooking, to minimize loss of flavour and vitamin C.

◆ Serve fresh fruit whenever possible and, as soon as your baby is ready, raw vegetables, such as avocado, peeled and deseeded tomato, well-washed crisp lettuce, pieces of red or green sweet pepper or a stick of carrot large enough not to choke on.

Salt

◆ Salt should not be added to food for babies (see 'Foods to Avoid', p. 27).

Sugar

◆ Try not to add sugar to your baby's food (see 'Foods to Avoid', pp. 27–8).

Cooking baby food safely in advance

◆ Once cooked, cool quickly, within one and a half hours – stand in iced water if necessary – then refrigerate, covered, for up to 24 hours, or freeze (see 'Meals to Freeze', pp. 166–80).

◆ If it is to be reheated, steam, or heat between two plates over a pan of boiling water, until the food is piping hot right through.

◆ Food should be reheated only once.

◆ Remains of food in a baby's dish should be thrown away, as it may have become contaminated with bacteria.

Water for cooking and drinking

◆ Water for consumption should always be taken from the rising main, usually the kitchen cold water tap.

◆ For babies up to about 8 months of age, all water should be boiled before using.

◆ Where a water softener has been installed, it is safer to take water from the non-softened supply.

◆ Where there is a filter to reduce the levels of nitrate and lead in the water, the filtered water is safe for cooking, but should still be boiled until your baby is 8 months old. Check with the manufacturer before using filtered water for baby feeds.

◆ Avoid bottled water labelled 'natural mineral water', the mineral salts in which could put a strain on a baby's immature kidneys. Other bottled waters should be safe – but again, boil.

Aluminium pans and foil

◆ While there is no firm evidence that aluminium saucepans or foils are associated with health risks, aluminium does react with acidic foods like tomatoes and citrus fruits and could get into these foods. For safety, therefore, particularly for acidic foods, use stainless steel pans whenever possible and use covered dishes in place of foil, or a barrier-coated foil, made specially for these foods.

Microwave ovens

◆ These are ideal for speedy cooking, but recent reports suggest they are not as effective as conventional ovens in destroying food-poisoning bacteria.

◆ Uneven heating of food in microwave ovens may allow harmful bacteria to survive.

◆ For a baby, therefore, it is safer not to use microwave ovens to heat, cook or defrost risky foods like meat, poultry and eggs, or dishes containing these foods.

◆ Microwave defrosting or cooking for foods such as vegetables – particularly potatoes to be baked, fruits and pulses – is safe and healthy, as long as you follow the manufacturer's instructions and check that the food is cooked right through.

Pressure cookers

◆ Pressure-cooked food is safe and healthy, with minimum loss of nutrients if correctly cooked – follow the manufacturer's instructions.

◆ Cooking time is considerably reduced – sometimes by half – for foods such as pulses that can take hours by conventional methods.

◆ For babies, a complete meal – fish, meat or a nut roast, two veg and a pudding – can be cooked at once.

◆ Prestige and other manufacturers produce various sizes in stainless steel or aluminium.

FEEDING GUIDELINES

By Sally Parsonage, nutritionist and mother of two

INTRODUCING SOLID FOODS

Confusing advice and food scares

For the first few months, milk alone, whether breast or formula, provides everything your baby needs for ideal nutrition, all in one simple food. When he is ready to start on solid foods, however, you will have to make decisions about what to give him. This has never been easy, with a mass of confusing information and advice from food manufacturers, health visitors and the media, not to mention well-meaning friends and relations. Today, with the never-ending succession of 'food scares', it has become even harder to be confident that your baby is getting a safe and healthy diet at every stage.

Ensuring a healthy diet

Some of the issues you need to know about, like choosing food wisely, safe storage and preparation, and sound kitchen hygiene, have already been dealt with. Others, concerned with when to start and which solid foods to give your baby, from first tastes to a full well-balanced diet, are dealt with here.

Let your baby guide you

Most babies are ready for a little solid food somewhere between 3 and 6 months – earlier than this the baby's digestive system is really not ready to deal with anything other than milk. Your baby may show when she is ready for solids by still being hungry after a normal milk feed, or by wanting to feed more often than usual. If you are unsure, talk to your health visitor. By about 6 months of age a baby's nutritional needs are greater and milk alone will not be adequate for much longer.

When and what to start with

Start by offering a little puréed vegetable, fruit, or cereal (see

'Purées Galore', pp. 65–90), on the tip of a small, clean teaspoon. The best time to try is after a daytime milk feed when you are both fairly relaxed and have plenty of time. If she seems to take to the idea, offer a little more, but two or three teaspoonfuls is quite enough for a first time. If, on the other hand, she gets upset or just does not seem interested, leave it for a few days before trying again, perhaps with a different purée.

One new food at a time

Once your baby has got used to the idea of solid food you can gradually introduce it after other daytime milk feeds. You can also try new foods one at a time in purée form – you will find that your baby quickly shows which she likes and which she does not! At this stage, milk, either breast or formula, is still the mainstay of your baby's diet, and solids are really just a little 'extra' to get her used to the idea of food from a spoon.

THE NEXT STAGE
Replacing milk

Once your baby is happily taking a little solid food at several feeds you can start to replace some of his daily milk intake with other foods. Begin by offering solid food before the milk at one feed, and once he is eating a reasonable amount of food, try offering a drink of cooled, boiled water or very dilute fruit juice instead of the milk. Some babies are quite happy with this arrangement, while others will still demand milk. Be guided by your baby. The last feed of the evening, and any night-time feeds, are best kept as milk-only feeds.

Avoiding allergies

At this stage you can introduce more foods from the 'Purées' section (pp. 65–90), and experiment with combinations of foods like fruit purée mixed with a little soft cheese, or combine a pulse and a cereal purée. But don't be in too much of a hurry – too many new experiences can be confusing for a baby, and you do need to keep a watchful eye open for allergies which may appear at this age, so stick to the rule of 'one new food at a time' to be safe.

Ordinary cows' milk, citrus fruits, nuts and wheat are best avoided until your baby is at least 6 months old, and egg white until 8 months old, as these foods can cause food allergies in young babies. Strawberries are best avoided until the second year. If a particular food does not seem to agree with your baby, don't worry, but try him with it again in a few months and you may find there is no problem. Many allergies of babyhood disappear by 5 or 6 years old.

Sense about sugar and salt

Don't add sugar or salt to any food you prepare for your baby, even if it tastes impossibly bland to you – remember, a baby's taste buds are far more sensitive than yours! Too much sugar contributes to tooth decay and offers poor nutritional value to a growing baby. Unfortunately, babies can become as fond of sweet food as anyone else so it is best to prevent a sweet tooth from developing. (Recipes that may need a little added sweetness include tips on what to use.) Salt puts an extra load on a baby's immature kidneys and should never be added – every food contains a little naturally and that is quite sufficient.

Suitable drinks

As your baby eats more solid food and has less milk, he will need more to drink. Cooled boiled water is the best, or *very* well diluted fruit juice, either from a bottle or a spouted cup. Avoid syrupy drinks that are high in sugar and are potentially damaging even to teeth that have not yet emerged (see also p. 18 for fruit drinks to avoid).

ON TO A WIDER VARIETY
Small meals

In next to no time you can start trying out some of the recipes for breakfasts, main courses, puddings, teatime treats and quick meals. Between 6 and 8 months is an important time to introduce your baby to new tastes and textures, and she will quickly learn to chew soft lumps of food, even though she may not yet have more than one or two teeth. You will not need to purée food to such a runny consistency, and thorough mashing with a fork or mincing will be adequate. If your baby objects at first, leave it, then try again in a few days' time.

Learning to chew

Chewing is an important skill which babies learn best at this stage – if they don't get the opportunity to try, it is much harder to learn when they are older. Obviously it is important that any lumps of food are small and soft, like roughly mashed cooked potato, carrot or peas, to avoid the danger of choking. To guard against this you should never leave a baby unattended when she is eating or drinking.

Feeding themselves

At about the same time as babies start to chew soft foods you can introduce 'finger' foods which they can hold themselves and chew on, such as fingers of peeled apple or carrot, or toast (see 'Finger Foods and Teatime Treats', pp. 142–51, for more ideas). As traditional rusks contain a surprising amount of sugar, it is much better if you can make your own (p. 146) or use melba toasts or bread sticks. Once your baby gets the hang of finger foods it is a short step to trying to feed herself at mealtimes. First attempts will use hands rather than a spoon and will inevitably be messy, but getting the food from bowl to mouth will soon progress from being a joint effort to a solo one!

FEEDING STAGES

No two babies progress at the same speed, so do not worry if your offspring does not conform to the pattern outlined opposite, which is a rough guide to the needs of the 'average' baby.

WHICH FOODS FOR A BALANCED DIET?

A balanced diet is one that provides all the essential nutrients in the right amounts for the person consuming the diet. During the first year or two of life, babies grow faster than at any

0 to 3–4 months	Breast or baby formula milk provides complete nutrition. Cooled, boiled water can be given as an extra drink if necessary.
3 to 6 months	Introduce small tastes of solid food in purée form after milk feeds. Try new foods one at a time. Avoid egg white, wheat cereals, ordinary cows' milk, citrus fruits, strawberries and nuts. Milk is still the major part of the diet.
6 to 8 months	Solids can start to replace milk feeds. Introduce new tastes and textures of food. Baby can chew soft lumps and finger foods, and may try to feed himself. Give plenty of water or well-diluted fruit juice to drink; start giving vitamin drops.
8 to 12 months	Solid food now major part of diet, but still include ¾ to 1 pint of breast, formula or whole cows' milk every day. Food can be mashed or chopped finely now, and baby can start sharing family meals when suitable.

other time, so getting the right balance of nutrients is vital. But don't panic and reach for your calculator, because there are some very simple guidelines that you can follow to make sure that your baby is getting a well-balanced diet once he is established on solid food.

Are extra vitamins necessary?

A healthy baby who is beginning to eat a range of solid foods as well as breast or formula milk is extremely unlikely to be short of vitamins. But as a safeguard, the latest Government Report on Infant Feeding (DHSS 1988) advises giving babies extra vitamins A, C and D from 6 months up to 2 years old. These extra vitamins could be important if your baby has a small or fickle appetite, and will certainly help tide her over periods of illness when she will not want to eat much. Suitable vitamin drops are available from baby clinics or chemists' shops. It is essential that you give only the exact number of vitamin drops prescribed on the label, as too much can be as harmful as too little.

GUIDING PRINCIPLES

1. Every food contains a unique blend of nutrients, so the wider the variety of foods you give your baby, the more certain you can be that he is getting enough of all the necessary carbohydrates, proteins, vitamins and minerals.

2. While a particular food may be good for your baby, it does not necessarily follow that lots of it is even better for him, so you do need to practise moderation, and not go overboard with any one type of food.

You won't go far wrong if you follow these two principles, but as an additional safeguard, you can refer to 'Foods for a Balanced Diet', p. 54. This divides everyday foods into five main groups, according to the range of nutrients that they contain. All you have to do is check that your baby is getting at least one item from each group every day – if this is the case then you can rest assured that he is getting all the nutrients he needs for growth and health. As you can see, because each group contains a number of foods it is easy to find alternatives for foods that your baby dislikes, or which you do not wish him to eat for any reason, without reducing the nutritional

AVERAGE ENERGY NEEDS OF BABIES

Age	Calories per day	
	Boys	*Girls*
0–3 months	545	515
4–6 months	690	645
7–9 months	825	765
10–12 months	920	865
1–3 years	1230	1165
4–6 years	1750	1545
(*Adults*	*men* 2550	*women* 1940)

value of his diet. For example, if he suddenly goes off the idea of drinking milk you can substitute yoghurt or cheese, and vegetarian babies can concentrate on the eggs, pulses and nuts in place of meat and fish. But in any case, the more you vary which food you choose from each group, the better his diet will be.

ENERGY NEEDS
How much food is enough?
It is impossible to say precisely how much food babies should have because, like adults, their energy needs vary enormously. A normal day's food for one baby might be starvation level for another, so it is never wise to make comparisons between what your baby and another consumes, even if they are of similar age and size. It is important to remember that every food provides energy (calories) which is the basic essential for life, growth and health. In the 'Foods for a Balanced Diet' chart (see p. 54), you will find an indication of the portion size of different foods which will make a useful contribution to your baby's diet, but in practice you will find that the best guide to quantity is his appetite. Do not expect this to remain constant – like us, babies have hungry and not-so-hungry days, and

small things like a cold or an emerging tooth can easily affect appetite.

In terms of calories

Compared with adults, babies have surprisingly high energy needs. If a 10 stone (63 kg) adult needs around 2,200 calories a day, you might expect a baby weighing 1 stone (6.3 kg) only to need 220 calories, whereas they actually need nearer 800 calories a day! The table on p. 51 gives you some idea of how your baby's energy needs are going to increase dramatically during the first few years of life. Remember these figures are *averages*, which means that they do not necessarily hold for individual babies. Yours could well need a lot more or less than the average, and boys do not always need more food than girls, but these individual variations will be reflected in his or her appetite.

Healthy baby menus

There are innumerable ways of providing your baby with a daily diet which is both adequate in terms of energy and well balanced in terms of essential nutrients. To give you some idea of the variations that are possible, here are two possible menus for a day for a baby of 1–2 years old – both would provide enough calories for an 'average' baby of that age, and you can check, using the 'Foods for a Balanced Diet' chart, that both contain foods from all the food groups, and so are well balanced nutritionally.

Do remember that the quantities suggested here are only intended as a rough guide – if your baby eats significantly more or less it does not mean that she is over- or undereating, just that her food needs are different from average.

AVOIDING FATNESS

A little chubbiness is natural

A fat baby is obviously not healthy, but a skinny baby is not ideal either. A reasonable amount of body fat is important to babies as a reserve store of energy to help them over periods of

TWO POSSIBLE HEALTHY DAILY DIETS FOR A 1–2-YEAR-OLD:

Menu 1	Calories
1 pint (500 ml) milk (for whole day)	360
1 oz (25 g) wheat flakes	100
1 boiled egg	80
Fish pie (p. 94)	120
2 tablespoons spinach	20
Apple brown Betty (p. 152)	90
1 tablespoon natural yoghurt	15
2 slim slices bread	120
¼ oz (6 g) butter	60
1 oz (25 g) grated Edam cheese	90
1 finger Banana and date cake (p. 147)	80
½ satsuma	10
Apple juice, diluted	30
	TOTAL 1175

Menu 2	Calories
Quick yoghurt porridge (p. 141)	90
1 banana	80
Orange juice, diluted	30
Baked lentil roast (p. 128)	150
2 tablespoons Brussels sprouts	25
Blackcurrant yoghurt (p. 155)	90
1 soft wholemeal roll	140
2 teaspoons smooth peanut butter	70
1 Rice and apple cake (p. 147)	50
1 pear, peeled, cored and quartered	40
1 pint (500 ml) milk (for whole day)	360
	TOTAL 1125

FOODS FOR A BALANCED DIET. Include at least one serving from each group every day

FOOD GROUPS	NUTRITIONAL VALUE PROVIDED	SOME SUGGESTED TYPICAL SERVINGS FOR A 1-YEAR-OLD BABY
A All kinds of *lean* meat, offal, poultry, pulses (peas, beans and lentils), nuts and eggs.	Energy, protein, fat, B vitamins, vitamin D, iron.	2 oz (50 g) lamb e.g. Irish stew, p. 103 *or* 2 oz (50 g) chicken e.g. Chicken risotto, p. 101 *or* 2 oz (50 g) fish e.g. Cod in cheese sauce, p. 95 *or* 1 boiled egg, p. 116 *or* 2 oz (50 g) cooked pulses e.g. Dilly dahl, p. 132 *or* 2 oz (50 g) soya curd (tofu) e.g. Tofu orange sponge, p. 160
B Milk, all kinds of cheese (soft, white and hard), yoghurt and all similar milk products.	Energy, protein, fat, vitamin A, B vitamins, calcium.	¾ pint (375 ml) milk *or* 2 oz (50 g) soft white cheese (see p. 8) *or* 3 tablespoons yoghurt e.g. Blackcurrant yoghurt, p. 155 *or* 2 oz (50 g) hard cheese e.g. Cheese pudding, p. 121
C Bread, flour, rice, breakfast cereals and pasta.	Energy, protein, carbohydrate, B vitamins, iron, fibre.	2 slices bread (white or wholemeal) *or* 3 tablespoons cooked oatmeal e.g. Nursery muesli, p. 139 *or* 3 tablespoons cooked pasta e.g. Pasta pick-up, p. 145 *or* 3 tablespoons cooked rice, see p. 85 *or* 1 oz (25 g) wheat or cornflakes
D Butter, all kinds of margarine, low-fat spreads, all cooking oils and fats.	Energy, fat, vitamins A and D.	½ oz (12 g) butter or margarine e.g. on bread *or* 1 teaspoon oil e.g. in cooking
E All kinds of fruit and fruit juices; all kinds of vegetables, cooked and raw.	Energy, carbohydrate, vitamins A and C, B vitamins, iron, fibre.	4 oz (100 g) baked or boiled potato *or* 2 tablespoons leafy green vegetable e.g. spinach *or* 1 medium-sized carrot, cooked or raw *or* 1 small banana *or* ½ peeled satsuma *or* ¼ pint (125 ml) pure orange juice, well diluted

illness and recovery when they may not be able to eat much, and as insulation to help them keep warm. Most babies are 'well covered', or even a little chubby, in the months before they start to crawl or walk. As long as it is not an excessive amount of fat it will disappear rapidly once they get on the move.

Take advice if need be

If you think your baby is overweight, do consult your health visitor or doctor who will advise you if any action is necessary – you should never attempt to put your baby on any sort of 'slimming' diet unless under expert supervision.

Prevention

The best approach to overweight is to avoid it: not introducing solids before 3 months, avoiding too much sugar and fat by preparing your own foods, and not pressing your baby to 'eat everything up' once he has indicated that he has had enough, will all help to avoid too many calories, which are responsible for excess weight gain.

JOINING IN WITH FAMILY MEALS
Adapting your food

At some time between 8 and 12 months old your baby will have progressed to eating three meals a day, perhaps with a milk-only feed at bedtime. By now she will be used to quite a wide range of tastes and textures and no doubt will be showing her individuality in which foods she likes and dislikes. But the best news of all is that she will now be able to share most family meals – all you have to do is take out the baby's portion before you add ingredients that would be unsuitable for her (see 'Adapting Family Meals for a Baby', pp. 181–206).

HEALTHY EATING FOR LIFE
From babyhood onwards, the same general principles of healthy eating apply to all the family.

1. Avoid salt and sugar
You will already be in the habit of avoiding excess sugar and salt in your baby's food – that advice goes for the rest of the family too.

2. Cut down on fat
Current nutritional thinking also says that we need to cut down on the amount of fat we consume, which means choosing leaner cuts of meat, not eating too much hard cheese, going easy on butter, margarine, whole milk and cream, and adding as little fat in cooking as possible. The only exception to this is that skimmed milk is not suitable for children under 5 years old, because its low fat content means that it is lower in energy and lacks important vitamins, although semi-skimmed milk is acceptable from about 3 years upwards if the child is eating a varied diet.

3. Eat more starchy carbohydrate
To compensate for eating less fat, we need to consume more 'starchy-type' carbohydrates such as those found in bread, cereals, pasta, rice, potatoes, other root vegetables, pulses and nuts. You will find that these foods feature prominently in the recipes throughout the book, while fat is deliberately kept to a minimum, so you should not find the transition from baby-only to family meals too much of a change.

4. Include fibre – but not bran

Fibre has received a lot of attention recently, and certainly many adults probably do not get enough in their everyday diets. So adults and babies (from 6 months onwards) alike will benefit from regular inclusion in their diet of wholemeal bread, wholegrain cereals like Weetabix or instant porridge, wholegrain pasta and rice and plenty of fruit and vegetables. Adding bran to your food is unnecessary for adults and potentially harmful for a baby, as are bran-enriched foods.

5. Be flexible

Everyone is different. From a year upwards it is impossible to make 'hard-and-fast' rules about foods that may be unsuitable for your baby – very acid-tasting fruits like grapefruit, seed-containing berries such as strawberries and highly spiced foods like curry are probably best avoided, or given as very small tastes until you are sure that your baby can cope with them. But as with so many things, your own judgement and your baby's/family's taste are the ultimate guide.

MAKE MEALS FUN!

From the earliest first taste of solid food, through sharing family mealtimes, right up to 'grown-up' celebration meals, food is an experience that you and your child can really enjoy together. You will find that if you get pleasure from preparing wholesome and nutritious food for your baby, mealtimes will, on the whole, be happy and relaxed occasions for you both. Food is fun as well as being essential for life and health, and if this is learnt early on it will, like most eating habits, stick for a lifetime.

<u>Recipes</u>

WHAT ABOUT EQUIPMENT?

FOR MEASURING
Scales and a measuring jug are useful to avoid guesswork.

FOR FINE CHOPPING AND PURÉEING
A fork or fine sieve will purée many things, but something more effective is required for jobs like mincing meat, chopping nuts and liquidizing less soft foods. The choice includes the following:

Mini choppers – similar to a mini liquidizer, but most, like Philips Mini Chopper/Milk Shaker, will finely chop, mince and purée things like meat, nuts, apples, onions, pulses and other fruits and vegetables to perfection. Very easy to use and clean, will have a permanent place in the kitchen for recurring small, otherwise fiddly jobs.

Food processors – these are ideal for all-round family use, but usually too cumbersome and wasteful for food for one baby. A mini processor that fits inside the large mixing bowl of the Magimix gives you the best of both worlds. It chops, minces and so on, as smoothly as the mini chopper above.

Manual hand blenders – useful to purée small quantities, as there is a minimum of waste, and they are easy to clean. Handy for travelling, too, allowing most foods to be puréed at the table. Not powered by electricity, you do the work, winding blades over a fine metal or plastic mesh.

Electric hand blenders – hand-held goblet blenders are useful to purée (not chop) small quantities of softer foods. A miniature windmill-like hooded blade is immersed in food to be puréed – easy to clean and convenient to use at the table.

Available cordless – recharged with electricity when not in use – and with conventional flex, by Philips and Braun.
Electric liquidizers – excellent for puréeing many foods, but can be wasteful for small quantities. The mini chopper, above, may be preferable.

FOR COOKING

Small saucepan with a tight-fitting lid – preferably in stainless steel (for possible hazards associated with aluminium, see pp. 41–2).

Double saucepan or steamer – again, better in stainless steel, useful for gentle cooking of foods like fish and liver and for small casseroles of baby food.

Small casserole with lid – useful for baked or steamed dishes.

Heatproof plates – for gentle cooking of small quantities of food over boiling or simmering water and for covering open casseroles.

Pressure cooker – useful for cutting cooking times and for cooking a complete meal – fish, meat or nut roast, two or three veg and a pud for a baby, all in one pot. See manufacturer's instructions: Prestige, for instance, provide a helpful leaflet on cooking baby food and have stainless steel as well as aluminium models.

FOR OVERALL HYGIENE

Easy-to-clean tray or large bowl and boilable cotton/ linen towel – until your baby is about 7 months old, when he will have built up some resistance to infection, keep his cooking and eating equipment together, covered after washing, away from any possible contamination.

MEASUREMENTS AND ABBREVIATIONS

Ingredients are given in simple British Standard measurements, teaspoons, dessertspoons and tablespoons (rounded unless liquid or otherwise stated), or in imperial measurements followed by the approximate metric equivalent, e.g. 2 oz (50 g) or ½ pint (250 ml). Oven temperatures are given in Fahrenheit (°F) followed by Celsius, which is the same as centigrade (°C), and the equivalent gas number, e.g. 350 °F (180 °C), Gas 4.

As a check, and to help in multiplying recipes for bigger appetites, for more than one baby, or for bulk cooking to freeze, here are the conversions used:

Weight		*Liquid*	
½ oz	12g	1 fl oz	25 ml
1 oz	25 g	2 fl oz	50 ml
4 oz	100 g	8 fl oz	200 ml
8 oz	225 g	10 fl oz/½ pint	250 ml
12 oz	350 g	¾ pint	375 ml
1 lb	500 g	1 pint	500 ml
2 lb	1 kg	2 pints	1 litre
		1 teaspoon	5 ml
		1 dessertspoon	10 ml
		1 tablespoon	15 ml

RECICES

Oven temperature

°F	°C	Gas
225	110	¼
250	120	½
275	140	1
300	150	2
325	160	3
350	180	4
375	190	5
400	200	6
425	220	7
450	230	8
475	240	9

Distance

½ inch	1.5 cm
1 inch	3 cm
2 inches	6 cm
3 inches	8 cm

Abbreviations used

oz	ounce
lb	pound
g	gramme
kg	kilogramme
ml	millilitre
fl oz	fluid ounce
cm	centimetre
min	minute
hr	hour

INGREDIENTS

For further information and guidance on ingredients, refer to index.

PURÉES GALORE

This is the way to prepare foods for first tastes – from about 3 to 4 months of age – as advised in 'Feeding Guidelines' (pp. 45–57).

Quantities given are the minimum practical for one baby. Surpluses will be inevitable to begin with – see suggestions for using these up on p. 90.

VEGETABLE PURÉES

Aubergine or egg-plant

½ medium aubergine

Wash, remove seeds and slice aubergine diagonally. Bring about 1 inch (3 cm) water to the boil in a stainless steel saucepan, add aubergine, cover and simmer until tender, 10–15 mins. Drain, discarding surplus liquid and skin. Purée with a fork, or sieve.

Avocado

1 avocado

Choose a ripe avocado, one that yields to gentle pressure. Flesh should be creamy yellow, tinged with green, and tender. Wash, cut in half, leaving stone in one half. From the other, scoop out 2–3 tablespoons, mash with a fork, and add a little milk for a smooth purée.

An avocado is more expensive than many other vegetables, but it is perfect for babies – nutritious, ready to eat, soft in texture and combines well with other foods (see Easy avocado, p. 216).

With the stone left in place and a squeeze of lemon juice to prevent discoloration, any left-over avocado will keep in the fridge for a day.

Beetroot

1 small beetroot (buy ready-cooked, with no additives)

Slip skin off beetroot with fingers or a knife and cut off stalk end. Wash, and dry with kitchen paper. Mash with a fork and soften with milk.

Beetroot may show up in a baby's bowel movement, but it is harmless.

Broad bean

2 pods fresh or 6–8 frozen broad beans

Shell beans if fresh. Bring about 1 inch (3 cm) water to the boil in a saucepan, add beans, bring back to the boil and simmer, covered, until tender – 20–30 mins for fresh beans and 3–4 mins for frozen ones. Drain, saving liquid.

Mash beans with a fork, sieve or put through a hand blender. Soften with a little of the cooking liquid or milk.

Broccoli

2–3 sprigs broccoli, fresh or frozen

Wash well. Bring about 1 inch (3 cm) water to the boil. Add broccoli, bring back to the boil and simmer, covered, until cooked, about 15 mins (less if frozen) – a fork will slide easily into the stalk when done. Drain, saving liquid.

Mash with a fork until smooth or put through a hand blender. Soften with cooking liquid or milk.

Brussels sprout

4–5 small Brussels sprouts

Trim off any blemished outer leaves and the base of the stalk. Wash. Bring about 1 inch (3 cm) water to the boil, add sprouts, cover and simmer until tender, 7–12 mins. Drain, saving liquid.

Chop roughly and put through a hand blender. Soften with cooking liquid or milk.

Cabbage

3–4 oz (75–100 g) spring cabbage, white, green or red cabbage, or curly savoy

Wash and put into 1 inch (3 cm) boiling water. Simmer, covered, until tender, 10–15 mins. Drain, saving liquid.

Put through a hand blender and soften with cooking liquid or milk.

Carrot

1 medium carrot

Scrub well and peel. Slice and put into 1 inch (3 cm) boiling water. Simmer, covered, until cooked, 25–30 mins. Drain and mash with a fork.

When your baby is ready, at about 6–8 months, try finely grated prepared raw carrot.

Cauliflower

2–3 sprigs cauliflower

Prepare, cook and purée as for Broccoli (opposite).

Celeriac

1 small piece celeriac, 2–3 oz (50–75 g)

Prepare, cook and purée as for Parsnip (p. 70).

Celery

2–3 stalks celery

Wash and remove root end and leaves. Chop and put into 1 inch (3 cm) boiling water. Simmer, covered, until tender, 15–20 mins. Drain and put through a hand blender.

Courgette

1 small courgette

Wash and trim off stalk and any blemishes. Slice. Bring about 1 inch (3 cm) water to the boil, add courgette, and simmer, covered, until tender, about 15 mins. Drain, saving liquid.

Put through a hand blender, or mash with a fork, and soften with a little of the cooking liquid.

Cucumber

2-inch (6-cm) piece cucumber

Wash, peel, cut in half lengthways and remove seeds from cucumber. Grate finely or mash with a fork.

Fennel

½ small bulb fennel

Cut off hard base, remove any blemished outer layers and trim off feathery tops and stalks. Wash and divide fennel into quarters lengthways. Bring 1 inch (3 cm) water to the boil, add fennel, and simmer, covered, until tender, 5–8 mins. Drain, saving liquid.

Put through a hand blender and soften with a little cooking liquid. Offer the remaining liquid, cooled, as a drink.

The delicate aniseed flavour appeals to many palates. Add any left-over raw fennel, along with the feathery top, to an adult salad or the finger-feeding bowl of an older baby. Alternatively, serve it cooked, as an accompaniment to fish.

French or runner bean

4 pods French or runner beans, fresh or frozen

If fresh, first wash beans, top and tail, and remove any strings. Chop diagonally. Bring about 1 inch (3 cm) water to the boil, add beans and simmer, covered, until tender, 10–20 mins. For frozen beans, follow instructions on pack. Drain, saving liquid.

Put cooked beans through a hand blender and soften with a little cooking liquid.

Leek

1 small firm leek

Trim off root, blemished outer leaves and the coarse green tops. Remove any inner grit by cutting top of leek in half lengthways and washing it under running cold water, fanning out leaves. Cut into pieces about ¾ inch (2 cm).

Bring about 1 inch (3 cm) water to the boil, add prepared leek and simmer, covered, until tender, about 10–15 mins. Drain and put through a sieve or hand blender.

Mangetout or sugar pea

4–5 flat, young, tender pods

These sweet edible pods are at their best washed and eaten raw when your baby is able to chew.

For younger babies, prepare, cook and purée as for French or runner bean (p. 69).

Mushroom

2–3 medium mushrooms

Wash well, remove stalks, trim off any blemishes, peel and slice mushrooms lengthways. Bring about 1 inch (3 cm) water to the boil, add prepared mushrooms and simmer, covered, until tender, 15–20 mins. Drain, saving liquid.

Chop roughly then put through a sieve or hand blender. Add a little of the cooking liquid for a softer purée.

Parsnip

1 small parsnip

Wash and peel parsnip. Slice or dice. Bring about 1 inch (3 cm) water to the boil, add parsnip and simmer, covered, until tender, 15–30 mins. Drain, saving liquid.

Mash with a fork and soften with a little of the cooking liquid or milk.

Pea

4 tablespoons peas, fresh or frozen

Bring 1 inch (3 cm) water to the boil, add peas and simmer, covered, until tender, 7–10 mins for fresh peas, about 3 mins if frozen. Drain, saving liquid.

Put through a sieve or hand blender and soften with a little cooking liquid or milk.

Potato

1 medium potato

Wash, scrub potato clean, and remove any blemishes. Bring about 1 inch (3 cm) water to the boil, add potato and simmer, covered, until tender, 20–30 mins.

Alternatively, dry with kitchen paper, score all round with a knife and bake at 400 °F (200 °C), Gas 6, until soft when squeezed, 45–60 mins, or microwave according to manufacturer's recommendations.

Peel boiled potato or scoop flesh out of baked potato. Mash finely and add enough milk or water for a soft purée.

Spinach

4–5 leaves (2 oz, 50 g) fresh spinach or 3–4 mini portions frozen spinach
Small nut of butter or sunflower margarine for frozen spinach

If using fresh spinach, wash under running water to remove all grit, cut away any coarse stalks and simmer gently, in the washing water adhering to the leaves, until tender, 10–15 mins. Drain, pressing out moisture, and retain liquid. Chop roughly, put through a hand blender and soften with cooking liquid.

If using frozen spinach, put mini portions into a saucepan with a small nut of butter or margarine and heat gently, stirring frequently, until thawed, then cook for 3 mins. Add a little milk or water, if required, to soften.

Swede

3–4 oz (75–100 g) swede

Prepare, cook and purée as for Parsnip (p. 70).

Sweet corn

1 small cob of corn or 3–4 tablespoons sweet corn, frozen or canned

If using fresh corn, remove leaves and wash cob. Bring about 1 inch (3 cm) water to the boil and simmer, covered, until tender, 10–20 mins, depending on age. Drain, saving liquid, and strip corn off cob.

If using frozen corn, put into 1 inch (3 cm) boiling water and simmer, covered, until tender, 3–4 mins. Drain, saving liquid.

If using canned corn, drain, discarding liquid, and rinse under the cold tap. Heat if required.

To purée, sieve or put through a hand blender, discarding skins. Soften with a little cooking liquid, milk or water.

(See Banana and sweet corn custard, p. 222, for any left over.)

Sweet pepper

½ sweet pepper (red ones are particularly sweet)

Wash pepper, remove stalk, seeds and pith, and cut into cubes. In a stainless steel saucepan, bring about 1 inch (3 cm) water to the boil, add pepper and simmer, covered, until tender, about 5 mins. Drain, saving liquid.

Put through a hand blender or remove skin and mash, adding a little cooking liquid if necessary to soften.

As peppers have a high vitamin C content, offer them raw as soon as your baby can chew.

Sweet potato

1 small sweet potato

Prepare, cook and purée as for Potato (p. 71).

Sweet potato's creamier colour and slight sweetness, as well as its red skin and more knobbly appearance, distinguish it from ordinary potatoes. It makes an interesting change.

Tomato

1 tomato, fresh and ripe or canned

If using fresh tomato, wash, cover with boiling water, leave for 2 mins, drain and peel. Chop and put through a sieve, discarding seeds.

Alternatively, cut peeled tomato into quarters, remove seeds and put through a hand blender.

If using canned tomato, put through a sieve, discarding seeds and skin.

Turnip

1 small turnip

Prepare, cook and purée as for Parsnip (p. 70).

Vegetable marrow

1 thick slice vegetable marrow
1–2 tablespoons plain yoghurt or soft white cheese, or 1 tablespoon mild Cheddar cheese, grated (optional)

Peel marrow, cut away seeds and pith, and cube. Steam or put into 1 inch (3 cm) boiling water and simmer, covered, until tender, 10–15 mins. Drain, press out liquid and mash.

For a thicker purée, add yoghurt, soft white cheese or Cheddar.

FRUIT PURÉES

As many fruits are slightly acid, tart or sharp flavoured for a baby, try introducing them with a bland food your baby enjoys, as suggested in some of the recipes. Plain yoghurt, soft white cheese or a cereal, for instance, are delicious with real fruit purées.

Apple

1 small or ½ large eating apple or Bramley cooker

Wash, peel, core and quarter apple.

Bring 2–4 tablespoons water to the boil in a stainless steel saucepan, add apple and simmer until tender, 3–4 mins. Mash and serve. (Even a Bramley is delicious with no added sugar.)

To serve raw, finely grate prepared apple, or chop roughly and whizz in a liquidizer with 2–4 tablespoons water until smooth. Alternatively, put through a hand blender and add water to soften.

Apricot

5 apricots, fresh or dried

If using fresh apricots, prepare and purée as for Plum (p. 78).

If using dried apricots, wash well, cover with water and soak overnight in a stainless steel saucepan. Bring to the boil in the same water and simmer gently until tender, about 30 mins. Drain and save the juice.

Sieve or liquidize the cooked apricots. Add some cooking juice to soften purée, and offer the rest, well diluted with water, as a drink.

Banana

½ ripe banana

Peel and mash, adding a little milk for a softer purée.

Blackberry

2 heaped tablespoons (1 oz, 25 g) blackberries, fresh or frozen
¼ teaspoon honey or apple concentrate, or 1-inch (3-cm) piece
 banana, mashed, if a little sweetening is required
1–2 tablespoons plain yoghurt, soft white cheese or baby cereal
 (optional)

If fresh, discard any blemished berries and wash. Thaw frozen blackberries in the fridge or in a bowl over simmering water. Sieve, discarding seeds. If necessary, add just enough honey, apple concentrate or banana to take away any tartness. To thicken, add a food already accepted such as yoghurt, soft white cheese, baby cereal or more banana.

Blackcurrant

2 heaped tablespoons (1 oz, 25 g) blackcurrants, fresh or frozen
¼ teaspoon apple or blackcurrant concentrate, honey or 1-inch (3-
 cm) piece banana, mashed
1–2 tablespoons plain yoghurt, soft white cheese or baby cereal
 (optional)

If fresh, first pick over, removing any stalks or blemished berries, and wash. Bring 3 tablespoons water to the boil in a stainless steel saucepan, add blackcurrants and simmer until tender, 5–10 mins. Stir in just enough honey, fruit concentrate or banana to take away any tartness. Sieve, discarding skins and seeds, and thicken, if you wish, with a food already accepted such as plain yoghurt, soft white cheese or cereal.

Cherry

6–8 cherries

Wash cherries, peel, and remove stones, retaining juice. Mash flesh with a fork and mix with the juice.

Date

10 cooking or dessert dates (not sugar-rolled)

Remove any stones, cut into pieces and put dates and 6 tablespoons water into a stainless steel saucepan. Cook over a gentle heat until they have softened, 5–10 mins. Sieve or liquidize with cooking liquid.

This is very sweet on its own but good in combination with unacceptably tart fruits and other foods. Stored in a clean jar with a lid, it will keep in the fridge for a few days.

Fig

4 figs, fresh and ripe or dried
1–2 tablespoons plain yoghurt, soft white cheese, baby cereal or
  1-inch (3-cm) piece banana, mashed

Wash figs, fresh or dried, well. Cover dried figs with water and soak overnight. Bring to the boil in the same water and simmer until tender, about 20 mins. Drain, saving liquid.

Sieve figs, discarding seeds, stalks and any coarse skin. To introduce gently, add a food already accepted, such as one of the alternatives above.

Grape

6–8 grapes, green or black

Wash well, peel, halve and remove any seeds. Mash with a fork or put through a sieve.

Grapefruit

½ small or ¼ large grapefruit
¼ teaspoon honey or apple concentrate (optional)

Peel, remove pips and pith, and divide into segments. Whizz in a liquidizer, adding 1–2 tablespoons water if necessary. If too tart, add just enough honey or apple concentrate to make it acceptable.

Kiwi fruit

1 kiwi fruit

Choose a ripe fruit that is not shrunken or damaged. Wash, cut in half, remove seeds and scoop flesh out of skin. Mash with a fork.

Mango

1 small mango

Choose a ripe, sound fruit, one that yields to gentle pressure. Wash, cut in half lengthways and remove stone. Scoop flesh out of skin and mash with a fork.

Mango's pleasant creamy peach flavour usually appeals to babies; like other fruits it is rich in nutrients such as vitamins A and C.

Melon

1 wedge (about 3 oz, 75 g) ripe, soft melon

Wash, remove seeds, cut melon away from skin and dice. Mash with a fork or put through a sieve, saving any surplus juice for a drink.

Nectarine

1 ripe nectarine

Prepare and purée as for Peach (below).

Orange

½ sweet orange

Remove peel, pith and pips. Divide into segments. Whizz in a liquidizer, adding 1 or 2 tablespoons water if necessary, until pulped.

Peach

1 ripe peach

Wash and dry peach. Peel, halve, remove stone and mash with a fork.

Pear

1 small ripe pear

Wash, peel, quarter and remove core. Mash with a fork.

Plum

3–5 fresh, ripe plums or cooking plums
½–1 teaspoon date purée (p. 76), apple concentrate or honey

If using fresh plums, wash, peel, halve and remove stones. Mash with a fork or put through a sieve.

If using cooking plums, wash, halve and remove stones. Bring 4–5 tablespoons water to the boil in a stainless steel saucepan, add plums and simmer until tender, 15–20 mins. Stir in just enough date purée, apple concentrate or honey to counter tartness. Drain and sieve.

Thicken as for Blackberry purée (p. 75) if you wish – banana also combines well with plums.

Prune

4–6 prunes
1–2 tablespoons plain yoghurt, soft white cheese, baby cereal or
 1-inch (3-cm) piece banana, mashed (optional)

Wash prunes well and follow cooking instructions on pack, using a stainless steel saucepan. Alternatively, cover with cold water in a stainless steel saucepan and soak overnight. Bring to the boil in the same water and simmer until soft, 15–30 mins. Drain, saving juice for a drink (well diluted), remove stones and sieve or mash with a fork.

To introduce gently, add one of the optional ingredients that your baby already accepts.

Raisin or sultana

10–15 seedless raisins or sultanas

Wash well, cover with cold water in a stainless steel saucepan and soak overnight. Bring to the boil in the same water and simmer until plump and tender, 15–20 mins. Drain and sieve, or put through a hand blender.

Like all dried fruit, these purées are sweet on their own but combine well with more tart fruits or with plain yoghurt, soft white cheese or similar, bland-flavoured foods.

Raspberry

2 heaped tablespoons (1 oz, 25 g) raspberries, fresh or frozen
¼ teaspoon honey or apple concentrate or 1-inch (3-cm) piece
 banana, mashed, if sweetening is required
1–2 tablespoons plain yoghurt, soft white cheese or baby cereal
 (optional)

Prepare and purée as for Blackberry (p. 75).

Redcurrant

2 heaped tablespoons (1 oz, 25 g) redcurrants, fresh or
  frozen
¼ teaspoon honey or apple concentrate, or 1-inch (3-cm) piece
  banana, mashed, if sweetening is required
1–2 tablespoons plain yoghurt, soft white cheese or baby cereal
  (optional)

Prepare, cook and purée as for Blackcurrant (p. 75).

PULSES

Dried legumes are healthy and convenient first foods. They are
nutritious – containing protein and other essential nutrients – and
easy to purée. For a few young babies they are indigestible, so
wait until your baby is accepting a few fresh vegetables before
introducing them, and if they are not devoured eagerly first time,
keep offering at intervals of a week or two and try combined with
a fruit or vegetable your baby enjoys.

As some pulses take an hour or more to cook, if you have a
deep-freeze it makes sense to cook in bulk and freeze any you are
likely to use regularly (see 'Meals to Freeze', pp. 167–9). A
pressure cooker will speed up the cooking.

Aduki bean

2 tablespoons dried or 4 tablespoons pre-cooked aduki beans

Prepare, soak and cook as for Butter-bean (opposite) but the
final cooking of aduki beans should take only 30–40 mins.

Black-eyed bean

2 tablespoons dried or 4 tablespoons pre-cooked or canned black-
  eyed beans

Prepare, soak and cook as for Butter-bean (below), but the final cooking of black-eyed beans should take only about 45–60 mins.

Butter-bean

2 tablespoons dried or 4 tablespoons pre-cooked or canned butter-beans

If you have a freezer and are likely to use these often, consider cooking in bulk (see 'Meals to Freeze', pp. 167–9).

To cook dried butter-beans, wash and discard any extraneous bits or blemished beans. Then soak: either cover with plenty of cold water and leave overnight (8–10 hrs); or cover with cold water and bring to the boil, cook for 5 mins, remove from heat, cover, and leave to soak for 1 hr. Whichever way, drain the beans in a colander, discarding water, and rinse under the cold tap.

Cover soaked beans with plenty of fresh cold water in a saucepan, and bring to the boil. Skim off any scum and boil rapidly without a lid for 10 mins. Reduce heat, cover and simmer until soft, 1–1½ hrs. Strain, saving liquid.

If canned beans are used, drain, discard liquid and rinse beans under the cold tap before using. To heat – not necessary, but sometimes desirable – bring to the boil in fresh cold water, and simmer for 1–2 mins.

Put beans through a sieve or hand blender, or mash with a fork. Soften with 2–3 tablespoons of the cooking liquid, milk or water.

Chick-pea

2 tablespoons dried or 4 tablespoons pre-cooked or canned chick-peas

Prepare, soak and cook as for Butter-bean (above).

Haricot bean

2 tablespoons dried or 4 tablespoons pre-cooked or canned haricot beans

Prepare, soak and cook as for Butter-bean (p. 81), but the final cooking of haricot beans should take only 45–60 mins.

Lentil

2 tablespoons split red lentils, whole green or brown lentils

Wash and remove any grit or blemished lentils. Cover with cold water, twice their bulk, bring to the boil and skim off any scum. Reduce heat, cover with a lid and simmer until soft – up to 15 mins for red lentils, 30–40 mins for whole green or brown lentils. Drain, saving liquid, and mash, adding some cooking liquid if necessary.

Mung bean

4 tablespoons mung beans

Prepare, soak and cook as for Butter-bean (p. 81), but the final cooking of mung beans should take only 30–40 mins.

Pea

*2 tablespoons whole uncooked dried green peas or 4 tablespoons
pre-cooked dried peas*

Prepare, soak and cook as for Butter-bean (p. 81).

Red kidney bean

*2 tablespoons dried or 4 tablespoons pre-cooked or canned red
kidney beans*

Prepare, soak and cook as for Butter-bean (p. 81), but fast boil
red kidney beans in the open pan at the beginning of the
cooking for 15 mins, then simmer until tender, 1–1½ hrs.

Soya bean

*2 tablespoons dried or 4 tablespoons pre-cooked or canned soya
beans*

Prepare, soak and cook as for Butter-bean (p. 81), allowing a
longer time for final simmering – from 3–4 hrs. Cooking small
quantities is not usually practical (see 'Meals to Freeze',
pp. 167–8, if you have a deep-freeze).

As soya beans have a high protein content, equivalent to meat,
this purée, bland on its own, makes a nutritious addition to
soups, stews or baked dishes and converts fruit or vegetable
purées into substantial little meals.

Split pea

2 tablespoons split peas

Prepare, cook and purée as for Lentil (opposite), allowing up to
30–40 mins for final simmering.

CEREALS

Here are a few suggestions for nourishing home-made cereals, as alternatives to baby rice and similar processed infant cereals.

Rice

Rice is a healthy first choice. It is nutritious, easy to digest and, unlike other cereals, free from gluten, which can cause allergies in some babies. There are several types:

Brown wholegrain rice – slightly more nutritious than white rice and with a nutty flavour.

2 tablespoons uncooked or 4 tablespoons cooked brown rice (see
 pp. 169–70 for bulk cooking and freezing)
1–2 teaspoons milk or water

To cook, wash in a sieve under cold tap. Bring 6 tablespoons water to the boil, add rice, cover with a tightly fitting lid, stir once and simmer very gently until grains are tender, about 40 mins. The rice should have absorbed all the liquid.

Sieve, mash or put rice through a hand blender and add enough milk or water for a soft purée.

White long-grain rice – this is blander.
Prepare, cook and purée as for brown wholegrain rice, but simmer for only 13–15 mins.

Pudding rice – absorbs liquid well. See Baked rice and almonds (pp. 154–5), and omit the nuts if your baby is not yet having them.

Ground rice

1 teaspoon ground rice – brown, which is slightly more nutritious,
 or white
¼ pint (5 fl oz, 125 ml) milk

Mix ground rice with the milk a little at a time. Pour into a saucepan and bring to the boil, stirring. Simmer until cooked, 5–8 mins, stirring occasionally. Serve warm or cold.

Flaked rice – available from health food shops, takes less time to cook. See Almond rice (p. 218), and omit nuts for quick plain rice.

Oat porridge

1 tablespoon rolled porridge oats
6 tablespoons milk or water

Bring milk or water to the boil in a small saucepan. Sprinkle on the rolled oats and simmer, stirring, for 1 min. Leave to stand for 2–3 mins and add milk for a soft porridge.

Maizemeal/Cornmeal

2 teaspoons maizemeal or cornmeal (see p. 11)
¼ pint (5 fl oz, 125 ml) milk

Mix the maizemeal or cornmeal with a little of the milk to make a smooth paste. Boil the rest of the milk and stir in. Return to the pan, bring back to the boil then reduce heat and simmer, stirring constantly, until cooked, 8–10 mins.

Alternatively, bring back to the boil, stir until it thickens, 2–3 mins, turn into a small casserole and cover, then bake at 325 °F (160 °C), Gas 3, or steam, for 20–30 mins.

Millet

1 teaspoon millet flakes
¼ pint (5 fl oz, 125 ml) milk or water

This makes a change from oat porridge.

In a saucepan, mix the millet flakes with the milk or water a little at a time. Bring to the boil stirring, then simmer, stirring occasionally, until it thickens, 12–15 mins.

See also Quick yoghurt porridge and 'Some healthy manufactured products' in 'Baby Breakfasts', p. 141.

DAIRY FOOD PURÉES

Egg yolk
(for babies over about 6 months)

1 egg
1–2 teaspoons milk or water

Cover the egg with plenty of cold water in a small saucepan. Bring to the boil over a gentle heat to prevent shell from cracking, and boil for 12 mins, when yolk should be firm and yellow. Remove shell, halve, and mash yolk finely with a fork. Add enough milk or water for a creamy purée.

Because of possible allergic reactions to the white, offer only the egg yolk until your baby is about 8 months old.

Cottage cheese

2 teaspoons cottage cheese
1–2 teaspoons milk or water

If the cottage cheese is too lumpy for your baby at first, mash or sieve it before softening with the milk or water.

Soft white cheese (other than cottage cheese)

2 teaspoons soft white cheese (see pp. 7–8 for choice of cheese)
1–4 teaspoons milk or water

Add enough milk or water to the cheese to make a creamy purée.

This is good on its own or with vegetables, fruit purées or pasta, served cold, or heated gently in a stainless steel saucepan.

Cheddar cheese

½ oz (12 g) mild Cheddar cheese
1 tablespoon milk or water

Grate cheese finely, or put through a hand blender, and place in a heatproof bowl. Bring milk or water to the boil, add to cheese and stir until it melts.

Combined with Soft white cheese purée (opposite) or on its own, this makes a quick cheese addition to vegetables, pasta and other foods.

Yoghurt

2 teaspoons plain yoghurt (see p. 8 for choice of yoghurt)
2 teaspoons milk or water

Stir enough milk or water into the yoghurt to make a soft purée. Good on its own or combined with other foods such as fruit and vegetable purées.

FISH PURÉES

White fish

2–3 oz (50–75 g) fresh or frozen bone-free fish – cod, haddock,
 coley, plaice, whiting or sole
2 tablespoons milk or water

If fresh, first wash fish and dry with kitchen paper. Cook with the milk or water on a covered plate over a pan of gently boiling water until flakes separate easily, about 10 mins, or 15-20 mins for frozen fish. Drain, saving liquid.

Remove any skin, check for stray bones and purée with a fork, or put through a blender, adding cooking liquid for softness.

Salmon

1–3 oz (25–75 g) bone-free salmon, fresh or canned
3–6 tablespoons milk or water

If fresh, first wash fish and dry with kitchen paper. Cook with the milk or water on a covered plate over a pan of gently boiling water until flakes separate easily, 20-30 mins. Drain off liquid and retain, remove any skin and check for stray bones.

If using canned salmon, drain and remove bones and skin.

Mash salmon finely with a fork or put through a blender, adding cooking liquid to soften.

Tuna fish

1–3 oz (25–75 g) canned tuna fish in brine
3–6 tablespoons milk or water

Drain fish well and mash with a fork or put through a blender, adding milk or water to soften.

MEAT PURÉES

Quick lamb or beef

2–3 oz (50–75 g) lean roasting or grilling lamb or beef
1 tablespoon milk or water

Trim off any fat and shred raw lamb or beef finely by scraping it with a serrated steak knife, or mince finely. Cook with the milk or water on a covered plate over a pan of gently boiling water, until the meat changes colour, about 5 mins. Drain, saving liquid.

Purée in a blender, adding enough cooking liquid to soften.

Stewed beef or lamb

2–3 oz (50–75 g) lean stewing beef or lamb

Trim all fat off meat and cut into small pieces or mince. Place in saucepan, add water to just cover and bring to the boil slowly. Simmer, covered, until tender, 15–45 mins. Drain, saving liquid.

Purée in a blender, adding enough cooking liquid to soften.

Chicken or turkey

½ breast of chicken
1 tablespoon milk or water

Wash chicken, dry with kitchen paper and remove skin and any fat. Chop finely and cook, with the milk or water, on a covered plate over a pan of gently boiling water until chicken is thoroughly cooked – white and tender – 15–20 mins. Drain, saving liquid. Prepare and cook a piece of turkey similarly.

Purée in a blender, adding enough cooking liquid to soften.

Kidney

1 small lamb's kidney

Remove fat, skin and hard core from kidney. Wash and dry. Slice and bring to the boil, just covered with cold water. Simmer, covered, until tender, about 15 mins. Drain, saving liquid.

Purée in a blender, adding enough cooking liquid to mix and soften.

Liver

2–3 oz (50–75 g) lamb's or chicken's liver
1 tablespoon milk or water

Wash liver and dry with kitchen paper. Cut away any veins or skin and chop finely. Cook with the milk or water on a covered plate over a pan of gently boiling water until it is cooked – no sign of redness – about 5–8 mins.

Purée, with cooking liquid, in a blender, adding more milk or water for softness, if necessary.

USING UP LEFT-OVER PURÉES

Vegetables, pulses, rice and meat
◆ Add to family soups, stews and casseroles.
◆ Combine with egg, breadcrumbs, mashed potato and herbs for burgers.
◆ Beat meat purées with butter or margarine, seasoning and herbs or spices, for a spread or a pâté.
◆ Blend chick-pea, haricot bean or similar pulse purées with half their weight in tahini, a little crushed garlic and your favourite herbs, plus a little olive oil, for a quick hummus.
Fish
◆ Blend with an equal quantity of soft white cheese or plain yoghurt and a few drops of lemon juice for a fish dip or pâté.
◆ Add to mashed potato, with seasoning, for a fish cake.
Fruit
◆ Delicious with plain yoghurt or soft white cheese, poured over ice-cream, whisked with milk for a fruity shake, or set in a jelly.
Egg and cheese
◆ Stir into savoury sauces and soups just before serving or combine with butter, seasoning and herbs for a sandwich spread.

NUTRITIOUS FISH

Where a recipe specifies white fish as an ingredient, cod, haddock, coley, plaice, whiting or sole would all be appropriate. (See also p. 3.)

Fish chowder

2–3 oz (50–75 g) white fish (see above), fresh or frozen
1–2 oz (25–50 g) carrot, washed, peeled and diced
2–3 oz (50–75 g) potato, washed, peeled and diced
2 tablespoons milk

If fresh, first wash fish and dry with kitchen paper. Remove skin and any bones and cut into small pieces.

Bring about 1 inch (3 cm) water to the boil, add carrot, cover, and simmer for 5 mins. Add potato and continue simmering until both vegetables are tender, 10–15 mins. Add fish and, with water just below boiling, poach with vegetables until flakes separate easily, about 5 mins. Check fish for stray bones. Stir in milk, bring to the boil and remove from heat.

Either whizz in a liquidizer, mash, or serve as it is. Sprouts, peas, runner beans or another green vegetable go well with this for bigger appetites.

Fish and tomato casserole

2 tomatoes, fresh or canned
2–3 oz (50–75 g) bone-free white fish (see above), fresh or frozen
1–2 dessertspoons plain yoghurt or soft white cheese

Make a thickish purée with the tomatoes, as on p. 73.

If fresh, first wash fish and dry with kitchen paper.

Place fish in a lidded casserole (avoid aluminium), cover with the tomato purée, and bake at 350 °F (180 °C), Gas 4, or steam, until flakes separate easily with a fork; 25–30 mins for frozen fish, less for fresh fish.

Check fish for stray bones and remove any skin. Put through a hand blender, mash or flake, depending on feeding stage reached. Combine fish and tomato with the yoghurt or soft white cheese.

Fish with spinach and orange

2–3 oz (50–75 g) bone-free white fish (see p. 91), fresh or frozen
½ teaspoon arrowroot
3 tablespoons pure orange juice
4–5 mini portions frozen spinach
Small nut of butter or sunflower margarine
Pinch of nutmeg

If fresh, first wash fish and dry with kitchen paper. Cook it on a covered, heatproof plate over a pan of gently boiling water until flakes separate easily, about 10 mins for fresh fish, 15–20 mins for frozen. Check carefully for stray bones.

Mix arrowroot with 1–2 teaspoons of the orange juice then add the rest and bring to the boil in a stainless steel saucepan, stirring. Set on one side.

Heat mini portions of frozen spinach with the butter or margarine over a gentle heat, stirring frequently, until it has thawed. Stir in nutmeg and cook gently for 3–4 mins.

For a purée, whizz fish, spinach and orange sauce in a blender, or mash finely.

For older babies, place fish on a bed of spinach and top with the orange sauce.

Fish with oats and yoghurt

2–3 oz (50–75 g) bone-free white fish (see p. 91), fresh or frozen
3 tablespoons milk
3 heaped teaspoons Ready Brek or similar instant hot oat cereal
1 tablespoon yoghurt

If fresh, first wash fish and dry with kitchen paper. Cook it on a covered, heatproof plate over a pan of gently boiling water until flakes separate easily, about 10 mins for fresh fish, 15–20 mins for frozen. Remove skin and check for stray bones.

Bring milk to the boil. Pour over oat cereal and stir until thick and smooth. Add yoghurt.

Whizz fish with sauce in a blender until puréed.

For older babies, mash fish finely, or flake, before adding to the oat sauce.

Pasta with fish and tomato

2–3 oz (50–75 g) bone-free white fish (see p. 91), fresh or frozen
2 tablespoons small pasta – rings or spirals
2 tomatoes, fresh or canned, puréed (p. 73)
1 dessertspoon plain yoghurt

If fresh, first wash fish and dry with kitchen paper. Cook it on a covered, heatproof plate over a pan of gently boiling water until flakes separate easily, about 10 mins for fresh fish, 15–20 mins for frozen. Remove skin, check for stray bones and flake.

Cook pasta according to instructions on pack.

To serve hot, combine cooked fish, pasta and puréed tomato in a small stainless steel saucepan and bring to the boil, stirring. Remove from heat and add yoghurt. Whizz in a blender to purée for younger babies.

Nursery kedgeree

1 dessertspoon long-grain white rice or 2 dessertspoons cooked rice
1 dessertspoon freshly cooked bone-free white fish (see p. 91), or 1
  tablespoon canned tuna or salmon
1 tablespoon plain yoghurt
½ hard-boiled egg yolk

If raw, wash rice in a sieve under the cold tap. Bring 3 inches (8 cm) water to the boil, add rice, cover and simmer until tender, about 13 mins. Drain.

For young babies, purée cooked rice and fish in a hand blender or mash finely, before adding yoghurt. Heat, if you wish, in a saucepan, stirring, but do not boil. Sprinkle with egg yolk, or stir it in, before serving.

Fish pie

1 medium potato
2–3 oz (50–75 g) bone-free white fish (see p. 91), fresh or frozen
1 teaspoon mild Cheddar cheese, grated
1–2 tablespoons milk

Wash, peel and cube potato. Bring 1 inch (3 cm) water to the boil, add potato and simmer, covered, until tender, 15–20 mins.

If fresh, first wash fish and dry with kitchen paper. Cook it on a covered, heatproof plate over the simmering potatoes, until flakes separate easily, about 10 mins for fresh fish, 15–20 mins if frozen.

Drain potato, mash, and add grated cheese while still very hot. Remove any skin from fish, check for stray bones and flake.

For babies under about 6 months, put fish through a hand blender, mix with the cheesy potato and enough milk for a soft purée.

For older babies, mix fish with cheesy potato, adding milk

as necessary. Turn into a lightly oiled heatproof dish, fork over the top and pop under a medium grill until golden.

Serve with spinach or another green vegetable.

Cod in cheese sauce

2–3 oz (50–75 g) bone-free cod, fresh or frozen
1 tablespoon plain yoghurt
1 dessertspoon mild Cheddar cheese, grated

If fresh, first wash fish and dry with kitchen paper. Cover with water in a saucepan, bring to a simmer and poach (do not allow to boil) until flakes separate easily, about 10 mins for fresh fish, 15–20 mins for frozen. Drain, remove any skin and check for stray bones, then put through a hand blender, mash or flake, depending on feeding stage reached.

Mix yoghurt and grated cheese in a saucepan, stir and heat gently until cheese melts. Remove from heat and add fish.

For bigger appetites, serve with a root vegetable, such as mashed swede, and some greens.

Creamed fish and cauliflower

2–3 oz (50–75 g) bone-free white fish (see p. 91), fresh or frozen
2 tablespoons milk or water
2 sprigs cauliflower, washed
1–2 dessertspoons soft white cheese

If fresh, first wash fish and dry with kitchen paper. Cook with the milk or water on a covered, heatproof plate over a pan of gently boiling water until flakes separate easily, about 10 mins for fresh fish, 15–20 mins if frozen. Drain, saving liquid. Remove any skin and check for stray bones.

Wash cauliflower and simmer in a covered pan (below fish, if possible), in about 1 inch (3 cm) water, until cooked, 7–10 mins.

For babies under about 6 months, put fish and cauliflower

through a blender – mash or flake for older babies – then mix with white cheese and cooking liquid to give a creamy consistency.

Heat, if necessary, in a saucepan, but do not allow to boil.

Grilled fillet and peas

2–3 oz (50–75 g) fillet white fish (see p. 91), fresh or frozen
1 dessertspoon sunflower oil
4 tablespoons peas, fresh or frozen
1 dessertspoon milk

If fresh, first wash fish and dry with kitchen paper. Brush

lightly with oil. Preheat grill to medium and cook fish until flakes separate easily, about 4–5 mins each side, longer if frozen. Remove any skin and check for stray bones.

While fish is cooking, bring 1 inch (3 cm) water to the boil, add peas and cook until tender, about 10 mins if fresh or 3 mins if frozen.

For babies under about 6 months, purée fish and peas in a blender, adding a little milk for a soft consistency.

For older babies, mash or flake fish and serve with peas, mashed or whole.

Fish savoury

2 tablespoons freshly cooked white fish (see p. 91)
½ egg yolk or 1 teaspoon soya flour
2–4 teaspoons milk
½ teaspoon parsley, washed and finely chopped
1 tablespoon crushed Weetabix (about ⅓ of a biscuit)

Remove any skin and bones from the fish and put through a hand blender or mash finely. Beat egg and mix with 4 teaspoons milk, or mix soya flour to a smooth paste with two teaspoons milk.

Combine fish with egg or soya flour mixture, parsley and Weetabix. Turn into a lightly oiled casserole. Cover with foil and bake at 350 °F (180 °C), Gas 4, or steam, until firm and dry, 25–30 mins.

For younger babies, mix to a soft purée with milk.

Serve with tomatoes, peeled, deseeded and chopped, carrots, or a green vegetable.

Fish mousse

1 medium potato
2 tablespoons canned salmon or tuna, drained
Few drops lemon juice
2 tablespoons plain yoghurt

Wash potato. Bring 1 inch (3 cm) water to the boil, add potato, cover and simmer until tender, 20–30 mins. Peel and mash.

Remove any skin and bone from fish, mash and add to potato with the lemon juice and yoghurt. For very young babies, liquidize or put through a hand blender.

Serve hot or cold. To heat, turn into a small casserole, cover with a lid and steam for 20–30 mins.

Fish Florentine

2–3 oz (50–75 g) bone-free white fish (see p. 91), fresh or frozen
4–5 mini portions frozen spinach
Nut of butter or sunflower margarine
Pinch of nutmeg
1 tablespoon curd cheese or fromage frais

If fresh, first wash fish and dry with kitchen paper. Cook it on a covered, heatproof plate over a pan of gently boiling water until flakes separate easily, about 10 mins for fresh fish, 15–20 mins for frozen. Check for stray bones, remove skin and flake.

In a saucepan, heat the frozen mini portions of spinach with the butter or margarine, stirring frequently, until thawed. Add nutmeg and cook gently for 3–4 mins. Add white cheese and cooked fish and continue to heat gently, stirring, but do not allow to boil.

For very young babies, purée in a hand blender or a mini chopper.

Mini fish cakes

1 medium potato
2–3 oz (50–75 g) bone-free white fish (see p. 91), fresh or frozen
¼ teaspoon parsley, washed and finely chopped
2–3 drops lemon juice
Small nut of butter or sunflower margarine, melted
1 dessertspoon fine breadcrumbs or finely crushed Weetabix

Wash, peel and cube potato. Bring 1 inch (3 cm) water to the boil, add potato and simmer, covered, until tender, 15–20 mins. Drain and mash.

If fresh, first wash fish and dry with kitchen paper. Cook it on a covered, heatproof plate over the simmering potato, until flakes separate easily, about 10 mins for fresh fish, 15–20 mins for frozen. Check for stray bones.

Add fish, parsley and lemon juice to mashed potato. Form into small cakes, brush lightly with melted butter or margarine and coat with the crumbs. Heat grill to medium and cook until golden, 3–4 mins each side.

For babies under about 6 months, mash finely or put through a hand blender, adding a little milk for softness.

Dice for babies feeding themselves and serve with runner beans or broad beans.

CHOICE CHICKEN
AND MEAT DISHES

Chicken casserole

1 small carrot
1 small potato
½ stalk celery
2–3 oz (50–75 g) bone-free chicken – breast, wing or leg
7 tablespoons (4 fl oz, 100 ml) stock (pp. 111 or 117), or water
1 tablespoon frozen peas

Wash and peel carrot and potato. Slice carrot finely and cube potato. Wash and chop celery.

Wash and dry chicken. Remove any skin and fat, and cut into small pieces.

Bring potato, carrot, celery, chicken and stock or water to the boil in a small saucepan, covered. Simmer until chicken is thoroughly cooked and the vegetables are tender, 20–25 mins. Add peas and cook until tender, a further 3–4 mins. Drain, saving liquid.

For very young babies, put chicken and vegetables through blender, adding enough cooking liquid for a soft purée.

For older babies, chop or mash according to feeding stage reached, adding enough cooking liquid to moisten.

Creamed chicken and apricots

5 apricots, fresh or dried
2–3 oz (50–75 g) bone-free chicken – breast, wing or leg
1 tablespoon milk or water
1 tablespoon plain yoghurt

If using dried apricots, wash well, cover with water and soak overnight in a stainless steel saucepan. Bring to the boil in the same water and simmer gently until tender, about 30 mins. Drain, saving liquid.

If using fresh apricots, wash, peel, halve and remove stones.

Wash chicken and dry with kitchen paper. Remove skin and any fat. Cook with the milk or water on a covered, heatproof plate over a saucepan of gently boiling water until thoroughly cooked, 30–45 mins. Add apricots about halfway through cooking time.

For babies under about 6 months, put cooked chicken and apricots through a hand blender and stir in a little yoghurt and cooking liquid to soften.

For older babies, cut chicken and apricots to an acceptable size and mix with the yoghurt.

Chicken risotto

1 medium or 2 small mushrooms
1 tablespoon sweet corn, fresh, canned or frozen
2–3 oz (50–75 g) bone-free chicken – breast, wing or leg
¼ pint (5 fl oz, 125 ml) chicken or vegetable stock (pp. 111 or 117),
  or water
1 tablespoon long-grain white rice

Wash and chop mushrooms. If fresh, strip corn off cob; drain and rinse if canned. Wash chicken and dry with kitchen paper. Remove skin and any fat, and cut into small pieces.

Bring stock or water with rice, chicken, prepared mushrooms and sweet corn to the boil, lower heat and simmer until chicken is thoroughly cooked and white, about 20 mins. Drain, saving liquid.

For very young babies, whizz in a liquidizer with some of the cooking liquid.

For older babies, mash or serve as it is, with cooking liquid to moisten, if required.

Grilled chicken and Brussels sprouts

5–6 small Brussels sprouts
1 breast of chicken
Few drops sunflower oil
Pea-sized piece of butter or sunflower margarine

Wash sprouts well, trim away any blemished leaves and stalk base. Bring 1 inch (3 cm) water to the boil. Add sprouts, lower heat and simmer until tender, 7–12 mins. Drain.

Wash, dry and skin chicken. Smear lightly with oil and put under a medium grill, turning halfway, until thoroughly cooked and white right through, 4–5 mins each side.

For babies under about 6 months, chop grilled chicken and put through a hand blender. Chop and finely mash sprouts with the butter or margarine. Combine the two and serve.

For older babies, cut chicken to an acceptable size. Chop sprouts and stir in the butter or margarine.

When sprouts are not available, try cauliflower, celery, peas or runner beans.

Chicken and bean bake

2–3 oz (50–75 g) bone-free chicken – breast, wing or leg
¼ red pepper
1 tomato, fresh or canned, puréed (p. 73)
2 tablespoons red kidney beans, pre-cooked (p. 83) or canned,
  drained and rinsed
7 tablespoons (4 fl oz, 100 ml) stock (pp. 111 or 177), or water

Wash and dry chicken, remove any skin or fat and cut into small pieces. Wash pepper, trim off stalk, deseed and cube.

Put chicken, prepared pepper, kidney beans, puréed tomato and stock or water into a small casserole (avoid aluminium). Cover with lid and bake at 350 °F (180 °C), Gas 4, or steam, until chicken is thoroughly cooked and white, about 45–60 mins. Drain, saving liquid.

For very young babies, whizz chicken and vegetables in a blender with enough cooking liquid for a soft purée.

For older babies, mash or chop and moisten with cooking liquid.

Irish stew

2–3 oz (50–75 g) lean stewing lamb
1 small potato
1 small carrot
1 teaspoon grated onion for babies over about 8 months
1 teaspoon frozen peas

Trim away any fat and cut meat into small pieces. Wash potato and carrot, peel and slice thinly.

Put meat, potato, carrot, and onion if using, into a small saucepan in layers, finishing with potato. Add water to come halfway up. Bring to the boil, lower heat, cover and simmer gently until the meat is tender, 1–2 hrs. Add peas, bring back to the boil and simmer for a further 3 mins.

For babies under about 6 months, drain and keep liquid hot. Put meat through a hand blender. Finely mash or blend potato, carrot, peas and, if using, onion. Combine meat and vegetables, adding enough cooking liquid for a soft consistency.

For older babies, mash or chop according to feeding stage reached.

Lamb with lentils and tomatoes

2 canned tomatoes and ¼ pint (5 fl oz, 125 ml) juice from can
1 tablespoon brown or green lentils
2–3 oz (50–75 g) lean lamb

Sieve tomatoes, discarding seeds and skin. Wash lentils. Trim away any fat from lamb and cut into small pieces.

In a stainless steel pan, bring tomato juice, sieved tomatoes, lamb and lentils to the boil. Simmer gently, covered, until lamb is tender and cooked, 1–1¼ hrs.

Drain, saving the tomato liquid. Blend meat and lentils, adding enough of the cooking liquid to make a soft purée.

Grilled cutlet

1 small lamb chop
Dot of butter or sunflower margarine

Trim fat away from chop and discard. Wash chop and dry with kitchen paper. Brush lightly with butter or margarine and grill under a medium heat, turning halfway, until cooked and brown right through, 8–10 mins. Pour juices from grill pan into a cup. Cool, skim off and discard fat, and reheat in a saucepan.

For babies under about 7 months, cut meat from bone, put through a blender and mix with the cooking juices and a puréed vegetable such as peas, sprouts or carrots.

For older babies, cut meat from the bone, dice and moisten with meat juice. Serve with leeks, carrots, sprouts or peas, and mashed potato for bigger appetites.

Mince and lentil mash

2–3 oz (50–75 g) lean stewing beef or lamb
1 tablespoon red lentils
½ teaspoon grated onion for babies over about 8 months
Pinch of mixed herbs (optional)
1 medium carrot (optional – for bigger appetites)
½ slice wholemeal bread

Trim away any fat and mince meat in a food processor (or get your butcher to do this for you). Wash lentils. Wash carrot, if using, peel and slice.

Put meat, lentils, water, with onion, herbs and carrot, if

using, into a saucepan, stir to mix and bring to the boil. Lower heat and simmer until meat is tender, 25–30 mins. Remove crust from bread and crumble it into the meat mixture. Mash to mix.

For very young babies, purée in a blender, adding a little freshly boiled water, if necessary, to soften.

Serve with a green vegetable.

Shepherd's pie

Ingredients as for Mince and lentil mash (see opposite), plus:
1 small potato
Pinch of nutmeg
Small nut of butter or sunflower margarine
1–2 tablespoons milk

Make Mince and lentil mash and place in the base of casserole dish. Top with mashed potato, prepared and cooked as on p. 71, with the addition of nutmeg, butter or margarine, and milk. Fork over the top and pop under a medium grill until golden.

Serve with peas or another green vegetable.

Mince pudding

2–3 oz (50–75 g) lean beef or lamb
2 oz (50 g) parsnip, turnip or swede
2 oz (50 g) carrot
½ teaspoon grated onion for babies over about 8 months
Dot of butter or sunflower margarine

Trim away any fat and mince meat finely or cut very small. Wash, peel and dice turnip and carrot.

Combine minced meat, parsnip, carrot, onion, if including, and 2 tablespoons water and turn into a small, lightly buttered pudding basin or casserole. Cover with a lid or foil, stand in a saucepan and add water to come halfway up basin. Bring to the boil, lower heat and simmer until meat and vegetables are tender, about 1 hr.

For babies under about 6 months, put through a hand blender and add freshly boiled milk or water to soften.

For older babies, mash or not, according to feeding stage reached.

Taffy's stew

2–3 oz (50–75 g) lean beef
1 small carrot
1 small potato
1 tomato, fresh or canned
1 small stalk celery

Trim away any fat and cut beef into small pieces. Wash, peel and dice carrot and potato. Skin, deseed and chop tomato. Wash and chop celery.

Put beef and vegetables into a stainless steel saucepan, with enough water to just cover. Bring to the boil, lower heat, cover and simmer until meat and vegetables are tender, 20–30 mins.

For babies under about 6 months, drain, saving liquid. Put through a hand blender and mix with enough of the cooking liquid for a soft purée, or whizz in an electric blender.

For older babies, mash or not, according to feeding stage reached, and serve with any green vegetable from 'Purées Galore' (pp. 65–73).

Liver mash

2–3 oz (50–75 g) lamb's liver
1 medium potato
Few drops sunflower oil
2–3 tablespoons milk or water

Wash liver and dry with kitchen paper. Cut away any veins and skin and put liver through a blender, or pulp it by scraping and pressing with a knife.

Wash potato. Bring about 1 inch (3 cm) water to the boil, add potato and simmer, covered, until tender, 20–30 mins. Cook pulped liver on a lightly oiled plate over the potato, covered with the lid, for the last 5 mins of the potato's cooking time, or until the liver changes colour.

Peel and mash the potato. Put liver through a hand blender. Combine the two with enough freshly boiled milk or water for a soft purée.

Serve with a puréed green vegetable or tomatoes, either puréed or peeled, deseeded and chopped.

Liver casserole

1 small carrot
½ small turnip
1 slice swede (2–3 oz, 50–75 g)
1 dessertspoon grated onion for babies over about 8 months
2–3 oz (50–75 g) lamb's liver

Wash, peel and dice carrot, turnip and swede. Put these, with onion, if using, into a saucepan with 1 inch (3 cm) boiling water, cover and simmer until tender, 25–30 mins.

Wash liver and dry with kitchen paper, cut away any veins or skin, and dice it. Add to vegetables during last 10 mins of cooking time, allowing it to change colour. Drain and keep cooking liquid hot.

For babies under about 6 months, put through a hand blender and add enough cooking liquid for a soft consistency.

For older babies, mash or chop according to feeding stage reached.

Liver and beef pâté
(for babies over about 8 months)

2 oz (50 g) lamb's liver
2 oz (50 g) lean beef
1 small carrot
1 teaspoon grated onion
1 tablespoon wholemeal breadcrumbs
1 teaspoon egg yolk or 1 teaspoon tahini mixed with 2 teaspoons
  water

Wash liver and dry with kitchen paper. Cut away any veins or skin. Trim away any fat from beef. Mince liver and beef or chop finely. Wash, peel and grate carrot.

Combine liver, beef, carrot, onion, breadcrumbs and egg yolk or tahini paste. Spoon into a lightly oiled casserole, cover with lid or foil, and bake at 350 °F (180 °C), Gas 4, or steam, until meat is tender, about 1 hr.

Serve sliced or diced with spinach or peas. (Liver rejected in other forms is often accepted this way.)

Liver cheese

2–3 oz (50–75 g) lamb's liver
1 medium potato
1 dessertspoon cottage cheese, soft white cheese or mild Cheddar
  cheese, grated

Prepare, cook and purée liver and potato as for Liver mash, p. 106.

For babies under about 6 months, purée the cheese as on pp. 86–7, and stir into liver and potato.

For older babies, stir cheese into the liver mixture without puréeing. (The cheese gives the liver an interesting lift in flavour.)

Liver and tomato

2 tomatoes, fresh or canned, puréed (p. 73)
2–3 oz (50–75 g) lamb's liver
½–1 teaspoon baby rice

Wash liver and dry with kitchen paper. Cut away any veins or skin and chop into small pieces. Put into a stainless steel saucepan with the puréed tomatoes and 2 tablespoons water. Bring to the boil slowly, then simmer until the liver has changed colour right through, 8–10 mins. Drain and keep cooking liquid hot.

For babies under about 6 months, put through a hand blender and mix with enough of the cooking juices and baby rice for a soft consistency.

For older babies, add baby rice to cooking liquid to thicken. Mash or chop according to feeding stage reached, add to sauce, and serve with spinach, cabbage or another green vegetable.

Kidney ragout

1 small potato
1 medium or 2 small mushrooms
1 tomato, fresh or canned
1 lamb's kidney

Wash, peel and cube potato. Wash, peel and slice mushrooms. Wash, peel, deseed and chop tomato.

Wash kidney and dry with kitchen paper. Remove any fat, skin and hard core. Slice, and put in a stainless steel saucepan with the prepared potato, mushrooms and tomato. Add cold water to just cover food, bring to the boil, lower heat and simmer until kidney and vegetables are tender, 15–20 mins. Drain, saving liquid.

For babies under about 6 months, put through a hand blender and mix with enough of the cooking liquid to make a soft purée.

For older babies, mash or chop according to feeding stage reached and serve with a green vegetable.

Kidney and beef pâté
(for babies over about 8 months)

1 small lamb's kidney
2 oz (50 g) lean beef
1 heaped tablespoon wholemeal breadcrumbs or crushed Weetabix
1 tomato, fresh or canned, puréed (p. 73)
1 teaspoon grated onion
1 teaspoon egg yolk or 1 teaspoon tahini mixed with 2 teaspoons
  water
Few drops sunflower oil

Wash kidney and dry with kitchen paper. Remove any fat, skin and hard core. Trim any fat away from beef. Mince beef and kidney or cut into small pieces.

Combine minced meat with the crumbs or crushed Weetabix, puréed tomato, onion, egg yolk or tahini paste. Turn into a lightly oiled lidded casserole (avoid aluminium) and bake at 350 °F (180 °C), Gas 4, or steam, until meat is tender, about 1 hr.

Serve sliced or diced with a green vegetable.

SIMPLE SOUPS

*Soups can be a healthy way of drinking nourishment –
serve in a cup when your baby is ready.*

SMALL STOCKS

Avoid commercially produced stocks and cubes as they are too
salty and highly flavoured for babies.

There are various easy ways of providing stock for a baby.
For instance, when making stock for the family, take out a
small portion before adding seasoning, onion, herbs, spices
and other strong flavouring. If you have a freezer, see Baby
bone stock and Baby vegetable stock, in 'Mcals to Freeze',
p. 177.

Alternatively, arrange to take some stock from your family
cooking:

From grilled or roast meat – make sure the grill pan or roast
dish is clean and delay adding seasoning and any strong
flavouring. Remove meat when it is almost cooked, add 1–2
cups of water to the juices, mix well, take out a small quantity
for your baby and allow to cool. Season meat and finish cooking.

Skim fat off cooled liquid, strain if necessary, and bring to
the boil. Serve on its own or use as stock.

From a roast – delay adding seasoning or any strong flavouring and take meat out of the oven about two-thirds of the way
through the cooking time. Press a dessertspoon into the meat,
allow juices to run into it and pour into a cup to cool. Season
meat and finish cooking.

Skim fat off cooled liquid, strain if necessary, and add an
equivalent amount of water. Boil gently for a few moments

and serve as it is, or add to a soup and boil for a minute or two before serving.

From braised or stewed meat – omit seasoning and other strong flavouring and about three-quarters of the way through the cooking remove 3–4 tablespoons of the liquid and allow to cool. Add seasoning and any flavouring to the meat dish and finish cooking.

Skim fat off cooled liquid, strain if necessary, and bring to the boil for a moment or two. Serve as it is or use as stock.

From vegetable cooking – use any liquid in which vegetables, such as those in 'Purées Galore', have been cooked, including pulses, but excluding potatoes cooked in their skins. Season only after removing some for your baby.

Vegetable broth

½ cup mixed diced vegetables (carrot, swede, potato, celery, parsnip, turnip)
1 small piece cabbage (1–2 oz, 25–50 g), washed, shredded and cut into short pieces
¼ pint (5 fl oz, 125 ml) stock (pp. 111 or 117), or water
1 dessertspoon plain yoghurt

Simmer all vegetables in the stock or water, covered, until tender, 20–25 mins. Whizz in a liquidizer or put through a sieve, and add yoghurt. Reheat in the saucepan if necessary.

Cream of pea soup

5 tablespoons (3 fl oz, 75 ml) stock (pp. 111 or 117), or water
2 tablespoons (2 oz, 50 g) peas, freshly shelled or frozen
5 tablespoons (3 fl oz, 75 ml) milk

Bring stock or water to the boil, add peas and simmer until tender, 3–4 mins for frozen peas, 8–10 mins for fresh ones. Either whizz in a liquidizer with the milk or drain peas and put through a sieve, before returning to the cooking liquid and adding milk. Reheat soup until just boiling before serving.

Cream of tomato soup

2 large or 3 medium tomatoes
2 tablespoons stock (pp. 111 or 117) or water
2 tablespoons milk
1 tablespoon plain yoghurt

Wash tomatoes and cut into quarters. Put into a stainless steel saucepan with the stock or water and simmer until soft, 1–3 mins, depending on ripeness. Sieve, discarding skin and seeds. Add milk and reheat soup until just boiling. Stir in yoghurt before serving.

Lentil soup

2 tablespoons red lentils
1 small carrot
½ teaspoon grated onion for babies over about 8 months
⅜ pint (8 fl oz, 200 ml) stock (see pp. 111 or 117), or water
2–4 tablespoons milk

Wash lentils, bring to the boil in plenty of water, skim off any scum, drain and discard liquid. Wash, peel and chop carrot into small pieces.

Simmer lentils, carrot and onion, if using, in the water or stock, covered, until lentils are soft and carrots tender, 30–35 mins. Either sieve and add milk until soup reaches desired thickness, or liquidize with the milk. Bring back to the boil before serving.

Chicken and celery soup

2 oz (50 g) bone-free chicken – breast, wing or leg
1 stalk celery
½ teaspoon grated onion for babies over about 8 months
Pinch of thyme (optional)

Wash chicken and dry with kitchen paper, remove skin and dice. Clean celery and chop into small pieces.

Simmer chicken, celery, onion and thyme, if using, covered with water and a lid, until chicken is white and thoroughly cooked, and the vegetables tender, 20–30 mins.

Either whizz in a liquidizer until smooth, or put drained chicken and vegetables through a blender before returning to the cooking liquid. Bring back to the boil before serving.

Cream of carrot soup

1 medium carrot
5 tablespoons (3 fl oz, 75 ml) stock (see pp. 111 or 117), or water
¼ pint (5 fl oz, 125 ml) milk
½ teaspoon grated onion for babies over about 8 months

Wash, peel and slice carrot finely. Simmer, with onion if using, in stock or water until tender, 20–25 mins. Drain carrot and sieve or mash before returning to the liquid. Add milk until soup reaches desired thickness and reheat.

Cream of spinach soup

4–5 leaves (2 oz, 50 g) fresh spinach or 3–4 mini portions frozen
  spinach
Small nut of butter or sunflower margarine
Pinch of nutmeg
4–5 tablespoons (3 fl oz, 75 ml) milk
1 tablespoon plain yoghurt

Prepare, cook and purée spinach as on p. 71. Add nutmeg and milk and heat until just boiling. Stir in yoghurt.

Baby bortsch

1 small cooked beetroot, puréed (p. 66)
1 small tomato, puréed (p. 73)
¼ pint (5 fl oz, 125 ml) milk
1–2 drops lemon juice

Combine the beetroot and the tomato purées in a stainless steel saucepan and add the milk. Bring to the boil slowly, remove from heat and stir in lemon juice.

Serve warm or cold. For latter, chill quickly by standing in cold or iced water, then refrigerate.

Mini minestrone

1 small potato, washed, peeled and cubed
Piece carrot about 3 oz (75 g) washed, peeled and sliced
½ stalk celery, washed and chopped into small pieces
¾ pint (15 fl oz, 375 ml) stock (pp. 111 or 117), or water
1 teaspoon grated onion for babies over about 8 months
1 dessertspoon haricot beans, pre-cooked or canned (optional)
1 mini portion frozen spinach
1–2 tablespoons peas, frozen
1 dessertspoon wholewheat macaroni or other small pasta

Put prepared potato, carrot, celery, stock or water, into a saucepan with the onion and haricot beans, if using. Bring to the boil, lower heat and simmer for 20 mins. Add spinach, peas and pasta and continue simmering until pasta and vegetables are tender, a further 10–12 mins. Liquidize or put through a sieve before serving.

WAYS WITH EGGS

Eggs are an excellent source of nourishment but, sadly, no longer as safe as they were because of the widespread infection of laying flocks with salmonella. However, if cooked thoroughly, by methods that will ensure the destruction of any bacteria present in the eggs, they can still be eaten safely. In this section, as in egg options elsewhere, the cooking methods are as prescribed for safety by microbiologist Professor Richard Lacey* who was involved in exposing the seriousness of the hazards. For other egg cautions, see pp. 7, 32 and 40.

Boiled egg

1 egg

Cover egg with plenty of cold water in a small lidded saucepan. Bring to the boil over a gentle heat to prevent cracking and boil, covered, for 12 mins, when yolk should be firm and yellow. Cool by running cold water into the pan, and shell the egg.

For babies under about 8 months, use yolk only. Mash finely with a fork and mix to a soft purée with 1–2 teaspoons milk.

Serve on its own or, once your baby accepts it, mix with another purée such as a vegetable, a cereal, a pulse, rice, fish or soft white cheese.

* For further information see *Safe Shopping, Safe Cooking, Safe Eating* by Richard Lacey, Penguin, 1989.

For older babies, mash or chop whole egg for spoon- or finger-feeding.

Scrambled egg

1 egg – yolk only for babies under about 8 months
1 tablespoon milk or 2 tablespoons for yolk only
Small nut of butter or sunflower margarine

Beat egg and mix with the milk. Melt butter or margarine in a small heavy saucepan, stir in egg and milk. Cook gently, stirring, until it is firm and dry, about 5 mins.

Serve on its own or, for older babies, with toast.

Baked egg
(for babies over about 8 months)

1 egg
2 tablespoons milk

Beat the egg, add the milk, and pour into an ovenproof dish. Bake at 350 °F (180 °C), Gas 4, until firm and dry, when a knife inserted will come out clean, 35–40 mins.

Egg, cheese and vegetable bake
(for babies over about 8 months)

1 egg
3 tablespoons milk
1 dessertspoon mild Cheddar cheese, grated
2–3 slices freshly cooked potato or carrot
1 tomato, washed, peeled, deseeded and chopped

Beat the egg, add the milk and cheese. Put the vegetables in the bottom of an ovenproof dish and cover with the egg and cheese mixture. Bake at 350 °F (180 °C), Gas 4, until egg is firm and dry, when a knife inserted will come out clean, 35–40 mins.

Spinach scramble

1 egg – yolk only for babies under about 8 months
1 tablespoon milk
3 mini portions frozen spinach
Small nut of butter or sunflower margarine
Pinch of nutmeg (optional)

Beat egg and add milk.

Put mini portions of frozen spinach into a saucepan with the butter or margarine and heat gently, stirring frequently, until thawed. Add the beaten egg and milk, with nutmeg if including, and stir over a medium heat until mixture is firm and dry, with egg thoroughly cooked and set, about 5 mins.

This is a delicious combination and good with rice for bigger appetites.

Cheese custard

1 egg – yolk only for babies under about 8 months
1 tablespoon mild Cheddar cheese, grated
¼ pint (5 fl oz, 125 ml) milk
Dot of butter or sunflower margarine

Beat egg, add cheese, and stir in milk. Pour into a lightly buttered casserole, cover with foil and bake at 350 °F (180 °C), Gas 4, until firmly set and golden brown on top, or steam until firmly set, when a knife inserted will come out clean, 30–35 mins.

Vary this dish by adding a tomato – puréed, or peeled, deseeded and chopped – to the egg mixture before cooking. Use all the juice and slightly less milk.

VEGETARIAN FARE

These recipes are intended to be enjoyed by all babies – not just vegetarians. They cater for the growing aware- ness of the importance of plant and vegetable foods in our diet. Vegetables, pulses, cereals, fruit and nuts are wholesome healthy foods, mostly easier to digest than meat, and they can supply all the nutrients we need (see 'Feeding Guidelines', pp. 43–57).

For more ideas see 'Quick Meals' where most of the recipes are vegetarian and, like many in this section, some are vegan too, containing no animal products such as milk, cheese, eggs or yoghurt.

CHEESE CHOICE

Brown rice and spinach

4–5 leaves (2 oz, 50 g) fresh spinach or 3–4 mini portions frozen spinach
3 tablespoons (1½ oz, 40 g) cooked brown rice (p. 84)
1 tablespoon mild Cheddar cheese, grated
1 tablespoon plain yoghurt
Pinch of nutmeg

Prepare, cook and purée spinach as on p. 71.

Combine puréed spinach with rice, cheese, yoghurt and nutmeg. Turn into an ovenproof dish, cover with foil, and bake at 350 °F (180 °C), Gas 4, or steam, for 20 mins.

For babies under about 6 months, sieve, put through a hand blender or liquidize, adding a little freshly boiled milk or water to soften.

Cauliflower cheese

3–4 florets (3–4 oz, 75–100 g) cauliflower
2 tablespoons milk
1 heaped teaspoon Ready Brek or similar instant hot oat cereal,
 baby rice or another baby cereal
1 tablespoon mild Cheddar cheese, grated

Wash cauliflower. Bring about 1 inch (3 cm) water to the boil, add cauliflower and simmer until a fork will slide easily into the stalk, 7–10 mins. Drain, saving liquid.

Bring milk to the boil, add the cereal and stir. Remove from heat, add grated cheese and stir until it melts.

For babies under about 6 months, put cauliflower through a sieve or blender before adding to sauce, or liquidize cauliflower with the sauce.

For older babies, mash or chop cauliflower, cover with sauce and pop under a medium grill until golden, if this is likely to be appreciated.

Cheese pudding

½ egg, beaten – yolk only for babies under about 8 months – or 1
 teaspoon tahini
4 tablespoons milk
2 tablespoons wholemeal breadcrumbs
1 tablespoon mild Cheddar cheese, grated
Dot of butter or sunflower margarine
1–2 tablespoons additional milk for younger babies

Bring milk to the boil, pour over breadcrumbs and leave to soak for a few mins. Add cheese and egg or tahini and mix well. Turn into a lightly buttered casserole and cover with foil. Bake at 375 °F (190 °C), Gas 5, or steam, until firm and dry, when a knife inserted will come out clean, 35–40 mins.

For babies under about 6 months, bring milk to the boil and mix with pudding to soften.

For older babies serve hot or cold, diced for spoon- or finger-feeding.

Cottage bake

1 medium blemish-free potato
1 tablespoon cottage cheese or curd cheese or mild Cheddar cheese,
 grated
1–2 tablespoons milk

Although the potato is baked whole, the cheese quantity is for half a potato, which will be sufficient for most babies.

Wash and scrub potato well. Prick or score round the middle with a knife and bake until soft when squeezed gently – in a conventional oven at 400 °F (200 °C), Gas 6, allow 45–60 mins and in a microwave oven allow 8–10 mins, following manufacturer's recommendations.

If using cottage cheese, sieve to soften for very young babies. Cut cooked potato in half, scoop out the flesh, and mash with the cheese and enough milk for a soft purée.

For babies under about 6 months, serve as it is.

For an older baby, return mixture to the jacket, fork over the top and brown under a medium grill if this is likely to be appreciated. Allow a self-feeding baby to spoon out the cheesy filling and chew at the jacket, but keep a wary eye in case of choking.

Courgette au gratin

1 courgette
Pinch of sage (optional)
1 dessertspoon finely crushed Weetabix or oatcake
1 tablespoon mild Cheddar cheese, grated, or soft white cheese

Wash courgette, cut off stalk end and slice diagonally. Bring about 1 inch (3 cm) water to the boil, add courgette, and sage if using. Lower heat and simmer until tender, about 15 mins. Drain, saving liquid.

Sieve courgette, return to pan and add crushed Weetabix or oatcake, cheese and enough cooking liquid or milk for softness. Heat gently, stirring, without boiling.

Parsnip and orange

1 small parsnip
1 dessertspoon soft white cheese
1 teaspoon tahini (optional)
1–2 dessertspoons freshly squeezed orange juice

Cook and purée parsnip as on p. 70. Add soft white cheese, tahini if including, and enough orange juice for a soft purée.

Pommes pommes

1 small potato
¼ eating apple
Small nut of butter or sunflower margarine
1 dessertspoon mild Cheddar cheese, grated
3 tablespoons milk
1 dessertspoon ground almonds

Wash the potato. Bring 1 inch (3 cm) water to the boil, add potato and simmer, covered, until just tender, about 20 mins. Drain, peel and slice.

Wash, peel, core and thinly slice apple.

Lightly butter a small casserole (avoid aluminium), and cover the base with half of the potato slices, followed by a layer of apple slices, half of the cheese and dots of butter or margarine. Repeat, finishing with the cheese. Spoon milk over the top. Sprinkle with ground almonds, cover with foil and bake at 350 °F (180 °C), Gas 4, or steam, for 25–35 mins.

For older babies, if baking, remove foil halfway through cooking to allow top to turn golden.

For younger babies, mash and add milk to soften.

Potato casserole

1 medium potato
2 tomatoes
1 tablespoon mild Cheddar cheese, grated
Dot of butter or sunflower margarine
1 tablespoon milk

Wash, scrub, peel and slice potato thinly. Peel, deseed and chop tomato.

Put potato, tomato and cheese in layers in a lightly buttered, lidded casserole (avoid aluminium), finishing with the tomato. Spoon milk over, cover with lid or greaseproof paper, and bake at 375 °F (190 °C), Gas 5, or steam, until potatoes are cooked, 45–60 mins.

For babies under about 6 months, mash.

For older babies, chop.

Risotto

1 tomato
1 tablespoon long-grain white rice
1 heaped tablespoon mild Cheddar cheese, grated
1–2 teaspoons plain yoghurt (optional)

Peel, deseed and chop tomato into small pieces. Wash rice in a sieve under running cold water.

In a stainless steel saucepan, bring 3 tablespoons water to the boil, add rice and tomato. Simmer, covered, until rice is tender, 13–15 mins. Add cheese and yoghurt, if using. Stir over a gentle heat until the cheese melts, but do not allow to boil.

For babies under about 6 months, put through a hand blender or liquidize, adding a little freshly boiled milk if necessary.

NOURISHING NUTS

Mushroom medley

1 large or 2–3 small mushrooms
½ stalk celery, about 1 oz (25 g), washed and grated
½ teaspoon grated onion for babies over about 8 months
Pinch of thyme (optional)
3 teaspoons Ready Brek or similar instant hot oat cereal, or baby rice
7 tablespoons (4 fl oz, 100 ml) milk
3 teaspoons finely ground hazelnuts, cashews, almonds or peanuts

Wash mushrooms, peel, if necessary, and chop into small pieces.

Bring ½ inch (1.5 cm) water to the boil in a saucepan. Add prepared mushrooms, celery, onion and thyme, if using. Simmer until vegetables are soft, 20–25 mins. Drain, saving liquid.

Stir cereal and milk into the cooked vegetables. Return to the heat and bring to the boil, stirring. Add ground nuts and soften with cooking liquid.

For young babies, put through a blender or liquidize.

For older babies, serve with peas, beans or spinach.

Nut roast
(for babies over about 8 months)

1 tomato
1 teaspoon grated onion
Dot of butter or sunflower margarine
3 tablespoons wholemeal breadcrumbs
2 tablespoons finely ground hazelnuts, cashews or other nuts
½ egg yolk, beaten, or 1 dessertspoon tahini mixed with 1 tablespoon
  water
Pinch of nutmeg
Few drops sunflower oil

Cover tomato with boiling water, leave for 2 mins, drain, peel, deseed and chop.

In a stainless steel saucepan bring 5 tablespoons water to the boil, add the onion and tomato. Lower heat and simmer, covered, until onion is soft, 10–15 mins. Remove from heat. Stir in butter or margarine, breadcrumbs, ground nuts, egg or tahini paste, and nutmeg. Turn into a lightly oiled casserole, cover with a lid or greaseproof paper, and bake at 350 °F (180 °C), Gas 4, or steam, until firm and dry, about 45 mins.

Rice and nut roast

2 tablespoons uncooked or 4 tablespoons cooked long-grain white or
  brown rice
½ egg yolk or 2 teaspoons soya flour
2 oz (50 g) mushrooms
1 teaspoon grated onion for babies over about 8 months
2 tablespoons finely ground almonds or cashew nuts
2 teaspoons breadcrumbs or finely crushed Weetabix
Few drops sunflower oil

To cook rice, see p. 84. Beat egg yolk, if using. Wash, peel, and chop mushrooms finely.

Bring 4 tablespoons water to the boil, add mushrooms and onion, if using, and simmer for 20 mins. Remove pan from heat and add cooked rice, ground nuts, beaten egg or soya flour. Mix well and turn into a lightly oiled casserole. Sprinkle top with breadcrumbs or crushed Weetabix. Cover with foil and bake at 350 °F (180 °C), Gas 4, until firm, 30–35 mins.

For babies under about 6 months, sieve or put through a hand blender, and soften with a little freshly boiled milk.

Spinach and almonds

*4–5 leaves (2 oz, 50 g) fresh spinach or 3–4 mini portions frozen
  spinach*
Small nut of butter or sunflower margarine
1 heaped tablespoon cottage cheese or other soft white cheese
2 teaspoons ground almonds

Prepare, cook and purée spinach as on p. 71. Add the cheese
and ground almonds. Serve as it is, or heat gently, stirring, in
a saucepan, adding a little milk if necessary.

Soya nut savoury

1 tablespoon soya bean purée (p. 83)
1 tablespoon finely ground hazelnuts, cashews or other nuts
1 tablespoon tomato purée (p. 73)

Combine all three ingredients. Serve with puréed spinach,
peas or rice.

PEAS, BEANS AND LENTILS

Baby hummus

*2 tablespoons (2 oz, 50 g) chick-peas, canned or pre-cooked (see p.
  81)*
1 tablespoon tahini
1–2 drops lemon juice
2–3 tablespoons milk or water

If using canned chick-peas, first drain and rinse under cold
tap.

For younger babies, whizz chick-peas, tahini and lemon
juice in a liquidizer, adding enough water or milk to soften.

For finger-feeding, mash chick-peas with a fork, add tahini

and lemon juice. Serve as it is, or form into dice, accompanied by pieces of crisp lettuce, peeled and deseeded tomato or cucumber and plain rusks (p. 146).

Baked lentil roast

2 tablespoons dried or 4 tablespoons cooked red lentils
1 teaspoon egg yolk or 1 teaspoon tahini plus 2 teaspoons water or milk
1 teaspoon mild Cheddar cheese, grated
1 dessertspoon wholemeal breadcrumbs
Pinch of sage (optional)
Few drops sunflower oil

If uncooked, wash lentils, cover with water in a saucepan, bring to the boil and simmer gently, covered, until soft, 20–25 mins. Drain.

If using tahini, mix to a smooth paste with the water or milk.

Combine the cooked lentils with the cheese, breadcrumbs, sage if using, and egg or tahini paste. Mix well. Turn into a lightly oiled casserole, cover with foil and bake at 350 °F (180 °C), Gas 4, or steam, until firm, 30–40 mins.

Black-eyed bean casserole

1 small carrot
Piece parsnip, about 2 oz (50 g)
½ stalk celery, about 1 oz (25 g)
1 teaspoon grated onion for babies over about 8 months
5 tablespoons black-eyed beans, canned or pre-cooked (see pp. 80–81)

Wash, peel and dice carrot and parsnip. Wash and chop celery.

Bring 7 tablespoons (4 fl oz, 100 ml) water to the boil, add carrot, parsnip, celery, onion, if using, and black-eyed beans, and simmer until vegetables are tender, about 30 mins. Drain, saving liquid.

For babies under about 6 months, purée in a hand blender or liquidizer, with some of the cooking liquid.

For older babies, mash or serve as it is, moistened with cooking liquid.

Broad beans and chick-peas with almonds

2 tablespoons chick-peas, canned or pre-cooked (see p. 81)
1 tablespoon broad beans, fresh or frozen
2 teaspoons ground almonds
1–2 tablespoons milk (optional)

If using canned chick-peas, first drain and rinse under cold tap.

Bring 1 inch (3 cm) water to the boil in a saucepan, add beans, shelled if fresh, and simmer, covered, until tender, 20–30 mins for fresh beans, 4–5 mins for frozen ones. Drain, saving liquid.

Mash beans – easier if skins are slipped off and discarded – with the chick-peas and add ground almonds and either some of the bean cooking liquid or milk for a soft purée. Alternatively, whizz together in a liquidizer.

Butter-beans with mushrooms and cheese

4 small mushrooms
1 teaspoon grated onion for babies over about 8 months
4 tablespoons butter-beans, canned or pre-cooked (see p. 81)
2 tablespoons wholemeal breadcrumbs or crushed Weetabix
1–2 tablespoons milk (optional)
2 tablespoons mild Cheddar cheese, grated

Wash mushrooms and chop finely. Bring ½ inch (1.5 cm) water to the boil, add mushrooms and onion, if using, and simmer until soft, about 20 mins. Drain, saving liquid.

Mix cooked mushrooms and onion with butter-beans, breadcrumbs or crushed Weetabix and enough cooking liquid or milk for a soft purée. Bring back to the boil, and simmer for 1 min. Remove from heat and stir in cheese until melted.

For very young babies, purée in a blender, with added cooking liquid or milk, if necessary.

For older babies with big appetites, serve with peas, runner beans or spinach.

Butter-bean loaf

5 tablespoons butter-beans, canned or pre-cooked (see p. 81)
½ egg – yolk only for babies under about 8 months – or 1 heaped
  tablespoon mild Cheddar cheese, grated
1 tablespoon finely crushed cornflakes
1 teaspoon tomato purée (p. 73)
1–2 tablespoons milk or water
Few drops sunflower oil

If using canned butter-beans, first drain and rinse under cold tap.

Mash or liquidize beans with the egg or cheese, crushed cornflakes, tomato purée and 1–2 tablespoons milk or water to mix. Turn into a lightly oiled casserole (avoid aluminium), cover with lid or greaseproof paper and bake at 350 °F (180 °C), Gas 4, or steam, until firm and dry, about 35 mins.

For babies under about 6 months, mix with a little freshly boiled milk to soften.

Butter-bean and almond delight

4 tablespoons butter-beans, canned or pre-cooked (see p. 81)
1 tablespoon ground almonds
1 tablespoon milk

If using canned butter-beans, first drain and rinse under the cold tap.

Mash beans and mix with almonds and milk. Delicious and nutritious on its own, or combined with a puréed vegetable or fruit.

Cauliflower and lentils

1 tablespoon split red lentils
2–3 sprigs cauliflower
4 tablespoons milk
¼ teaspoon finely chopped mint (optional)
Pinch of dill (optional)
1 tablespoon cottage cheese or other soft white cheese

Wash lentils, cover with water in a small saucepan, and bring to the boil. Skim off any scum and leave to soak for a few mins. Drain and rinse.

Wash cauliflower and break into small sprigs. Bring 4 tablespoons water and the milk to the boil, add cauliflower, lentils, dill and mint, if using, and simmer very gently, half covered with lid, until a fork will slide easily into the cauliflower stalks, 20–25 mins. Drain, saving liquid.

For babies under about 6 months, mash cauliflower and lentils finely, or put through a hand blender, add white cheese and, if necessary, soften with cooking liquid.

For older babies, mash or chop cauliflower and lentil mixture, add cheese and a little cooking liquid, if required, to moisten. Serve with carrot, peas or beans.

For smaller appetites, omit the cheese.

Chick-pea hotpot

1 small carrot
2–3 oz (50–75 g) piece swede
½ eating apple
5 tablespoons chick-peas, canned or pre-cooked (see p. 81)

Wash, peel and dice carrot and swede. Wash, peel, core and chop apple. If using canned chick-peas, first drain and rinse.

In a stainless steel saucepan, bring 4 fl oz (100 ml) water to the boil, add carrot and swede and simmer, covered, for 10 mins. Add apple and chick-peas. Continue simmering until vegetables are tender, 10–15 mins.

For babies under about 6 months, drain, saving liquid, and purée in a blender, adding enough cooking liquid to mix smoothly.

For older babies, mash, if necessary, and serve.

Dilly dahl

1 small carrot
2 tablespoons yellow split peas
Pinch of dill
2 teaspoons finely ground sunflower seeds (optional)

Wash, peel and grate carrot.

Wash split peas and bring to the boil in ⅓ pint (7 fl oz, 175 ml) water with the carrot and dill. Lower heat and simmer until soft, 25–30 mins. Drain, saving liquid.

Mash with a fork or liquidize, adding cooking liquid or milk for softness, and ground sunflower seeds, if using.

Serve with brown rice and tomatoes.

Haricot beans and tomatoes

3 tomatoes and all the juice from a 14 oz (400 g) can
1 small carrot
4 tablespoons haricot beans, canned or pre-cooked (see p. 81)
1 teaspoon grated onion for babies over about 8 months
Pinch of basil, thyme and ground clove (optional – for older babies)

Sieve tomatoes, discarding seeds and skin. Wash, peel and chop carrot into small pieces. If using canned beans, first drain and rinse under cold tap.

Into a stainless steel saucepan put beans, onion and flavourings if using, sieved tomatoes and enough juice to cover. Simmer, covered, until carrot and onion are tender, and juice has thickened, 25–30 mins.

For babies under about 6 months, drain, saving liquid. Mash finely, put through a hand blender, or whizz in a liquidizer, adding enough cooking liquid to soften.

For older babies, mash or not, according to feeding stage reached, and serve with spinach or another green vegetable.

Lentil and potato savoury

2 tablespoons green or brown lentils
1 small potato
1 tablespoon mild Cheddar cheese, grated, or soft white cheese, or 1
  tablespoon finely ground nuts or sunflower seeds
3–4 tablespoons milk

Wash lentils, cover with water in a saucepan, and bring to the boil. Skim off any scum, reduce heat and simmer, covered, until soft, 30–40 mins. Drain.

Wash potato. Bring 1 inch (3 cm) water to the boil, add potato and simmer until cooked, about 20 mins. Drain and peel.

Mash potato and add lentils, then cheese, ground nuts or seeds. Bring milk to the boil and add enough for a soft purée.

Lentil and tomato potage

2 tablespoons red lentils
2 tomatoes and 7 tablespoons (4 fl oz, 100 ml) juice from can
½ teaspoon grated onion for babies over about 8 months
1–2 tablespoons cottage cheese or soft white cheese

Wash lentils, cover with water in a saucepan, and bring to the boil. Skim off any scum and drain.

Sieve tomatoes, discarding seeds and skin.

Into a stainless steel saucepan put lentils, sieved tomatoes, onion, if using, and juice. Bring to the boil then simmer gently, covered, stirring occasionally, until lentils and onion are soft, 20–30 mins. Stir in cheese.

For very young babies, sieve.

Red bean bake
(for babies over about 8 months)

2 tablespoons red kidney beans, canned or pre-cooked (see p. 83)
2–3 oz (50–75 g) piece carrot
2–3 oz (50–75 g) piece parsnip
1 tomato
½ teaspoon onion
Few drops sunflower oil
1 tablespoon mild Cheddar cheese, grated
1 tablespoon fine wholemeal breadcrumbs

If using canned beans, first drain and rinse under cold tap. Wash, peel and dice carrot and parsnip. Peel, deseed and chop tomato.

In a stainless steel saucepan bring ¼ pint (5 fl oz, 125 ml) water to the boil and add prepared carrot, parsnip, tomato and onion, with the beans. Simmer until all vegetables are tender, 25–30 mins. Liquidize or mash and turn into a lightly oiled casserole (avoid aluminium). Sprinkle with cheese and crumbs and pop under a medium grill until golden.

Rice and bean feast

1 tablespoon uncooked or 2 tablespoons cooked rice
2 tablespoons broad beans or peas, frozen
2 tablespoons haricot beans, canned or pre-cooked (see p. 81)
2–4 tablespoons milk

To cook rice, see p. 84. Cook broad beans or peas according to instructions on pack. If using canned haricot beans, drain and rinse under cold tap.

For babies under about 8 months, put cooked rice, broad beans or peas, and haricot beans into a liquidizer with enough milk for a soft purée.

For older babies, combine ingredients and chop or mash as necessary.

Soya bean casserole

½ stalk celery
1 teaspoon grated onion for babies over about 8 months
Small nut of butter or sunflower margarine
4 tablespoons soya beans, canned or pre-cooked (see p. 83)
2 tablespoons sweet corn, canned or frozen
2 tomatoes, canned or fresh, puréed (p. 73) and made up to 4
  tablespoons liquid with tomato juice or water
Pinch of basil (optional)

Wash and chop celery. If using onion, sauté in the butter or margarine until soft, 5–7 mins.

Into a stainless steel saucepan put beans, sweet corn, tomato liquid, celery, basil and onion, if using. Bring to the boil and simmer, covered, for 45 mins. Drain, saving liquid.

For babies under about 6 months, put through a blender or sieve, adding some cooking liquid to soften.

For older babies, mash or not, according to feeding stage reached.

Soya bean loaf

½ eating apple
4 tablespoons soya beans, canned or pre-cooked (see p. 83)
2 tablespoons wholemeal breadcrumbs
*½ egg yolk or 2 teaspoons tahini or 1 tablespoon mild Cheddar
 cheese, grated*
*1 teaspoon grated onion for babies over about 8 months and small
 nut of margarine*
Pinch of dill and marjoram (optional)
Few drops sunflower oil
4 tablespoons milk or water

Wash, peel, core and chop apple. If using canned beans, first drain and rinse under cold tap. If using, sauté onion until soft.

Into a liquidizer put: soya beans, breadcrumbs, apple, egg yolk, tahini or grated cheese, herbs and onion if using, and enough milk or water to mix. Whizz until thoroughly blended. Turn into a lightly oiled casserole, cover with a lid or grease-proof paper and bake at 350 °F (180 °C), Gas 4, or steam, until firm, 35–40 mins.

For babies under about 6 months, mix to a soft purée with some freshly boiled milk.

For older babies, cut into pieces for spoon- or finger-feeding and serve with spinach or another green vegetable.

TEMPTING TOFU

Baked tofu and tomato

1 tomato
2 oz (50 g) tofu
2 teaspoons ground almonds
Few drops sunflower oil

Cover tomato with boiling water and leave for 2 mins. Drain, peel, quarter and deseed, retaining juice.

Drain tofu and pat dry with kitchen paper. Whizz tofu and tomato, with juice, in a liquidizer or mash with a fork. Turn into a small, lightly oiled casserole, sprinkle with almonds and bake at 350 °F (180 °C), Gas 4, until risen and golden.

For babies under about 6 months, add a little freshly boiled milk to soften, if necessary.

Spinach and tofu

1 teaspoon grated onion for babies over about 8 months
Small nut of butter or sunflower margarine
3–4 mini portions frozen spinach
1 oz (25 g) tofu
Pinch of nutmeg
Pinch of dill (optional)

Drain tofu, pat dry with kitchen paper and crumble with a fork.

If using onion, sauté in the butter until soft, 2–3 mins. Add mini portions of frozen spinach and stir frequently over a gentle heat until thawed. Cook gently for 2 mins. Add tofu, nutmeg and dill, if including, and stir over heat for a further minute.

Pasta with tofu sauce

1 tomato
1 oz (25 g) small wholemeal pasta – rings, spirals or macaroni
2 oz (50 g) tofu
1 tablespoon yoghurt
1 dessertspoon ground almonds

Cover tomato with boiling water and leave to stand for 2 mins. Drain, peel, quarter, deseed and chop roughly, retaining juice.

Cook pasta according to instructions on pack. Drain tofu and pat dry with kitchen paper.

Whizz tofu, yoghurt, tomato with juice, ground almonds and, for very young babies, the pasta too, in a liquidizer until smooth. Pour into a stainless steel saucepan and stir over a gentle heat, but do not allow to boil.

For older babies, serve pasta topped with sauce.

BABY BREAKFASTS

Fruit and cereal with milk make a good breakfast. But there is no reason why your baby should not have whatever he enjoys at other times of the day, provided it is wholesome and you are willing to prepare it.

Porridge with fruit

½ eating apple or equivalent-sized piece of Bramley cooker
6 tablespoons milk or water
1 tablespoon rolled porridge oats

Wash, peel, core and grate the apple.

In a stainless steel saucepan bring the milk or water to the boil. Sprinkle on the rolled oats and simmer, stirring occasionally, for 1 min. Add apple and cook, stirring, for a further 2–3 mins. Serve with milk or plain yoghurt.

Variations: in place of apple, use pear, or 2–3 tablespoons of puréed fruit from 'Purées Galore' (pp. 74–80), such as apricot, prunes, figs, dates or banana. Try also 2 teaspoons smooth nut butter, sunflower (seed) spread or tahini, stirred into the fruity porridge, before removing it from the heat.

Nursery muesli

1 tablespoon rolled porridge oats
1 tablespoon cashew nuts
1 teaspoon sunflower seeds
1 teaspoon sultanas
¼ eating apple or equivalent-sized piece of Bramley cooker
2–4 tablespoons milk

Whizz the rolled oats, nuts, sunflower seeds and sultanas in a liquidizer until finely ground. Wash, peel, core and grate the apple. Put it, with the ground mixture and ¼ pint (5 fl oz, 125 ml) water, into a stainless steel saucepan. Bring to the boil, stirring. Reduce the heat and, stirring occasionally, simmer for 5 mins. Mix with the milk and serve.

For older babies, serve ground, uncooked muesli with hot or cold milk.

(The first 4 ingredients could be replaced with 2–3 tablespoons from a packet of muesli with no added sugar.)

Fruity yoghurt

2–3 tablespoons plain yoghurt
3–4 tablespoons puréed or chopped fruit from 'Purées Galore' (pp. 74–80)

Mix and serve.
Variations: in place of yoghurt, use fromage frais or another soft white cheese, softened with milk if necessary.

Apricot mousse
(for babies over about 8 months)

3 dried apricots
3 tablespoons milk
2 tablespoons plain yoghurt (optional)

This thick fruity mousse is very easy to make, but requires time in the refrigerator. Prepared the night before, therefore, it makes a very good breakfast.

Wash apricots well and pat dry with kitchen paper. Chop finely or mince in a blender, spread evenly on the base of a small dish and cover with the milk. Refrigerate overnight, or for 6–8 hours, when it will have become thick and mousse-like. If adding yoghurt, stir in before serving.

Quick yoghurt porridge

4 tablespoons milk
1 heaped tablespoon Ready Brek or similar instant hot oat cereal
1 tablespoon plain yoghurt

Bring milk to the boil, pour over instant hot oat cereal, stir to mix and add yoghurt.

Optional extras:

◆ 1 tablespoon ground almonds
◆ fruit as for Porridge with fruit (p. 139)
◆ 1–2 teaspoons sugar-free pure fruit spread or smooth nut butter
◆ ¼ teaspoon pure fruit concentrate

OTHER IDEAS FOR BREAKFAST

Recipes

◆ Oat porridge (p. 85), or, for a change, Millet porridge (p. 85).
◆ Rice or another cereal from 'Purées Galore' (pp. 84–6).
◆ Egg, boiled, scrambled or baked as in 'Ways With Eggs' (pp. 116–17).
◆ Tomato and cheese – and variations – from 'Quick Meals' (pp. 212–13).
◆ Almond rice – and variations – from 'Quick Meals' (p. 218).

Some healthy manufactured products

◆ Sugar-free muesli from a packet, ground powder fine in a food processor and cooked as in Nursery muesli (p. 139).
◆ Ready Brek or similar instant hot oat cereal, in place of rolled oats, as in Porridge with fruit (p. 139).
◆ A Weetabix, Shredded Wheat, oatcake, salt-free rice cake or Ryvita from a packet, softened with freshly boiled milk, with added fruit as in Porridge with fruit (p. 139).

FINGER FOODS AND TEATIME TREATS

At about 6 or 7 months of age, when your baby shows signs of wanting to chew and to feed herself, it is important to encourage her. But constant supervision is essential – it is very easy to choke on a piece of lumpy food before learning to chew it soft and small enough to swallow comfortably. Let her help herself to food as soon as she wants to, be prepared for the mess until it all finds the mouth – and spoon-feeding will follow naturally.

VEGETABLES

Cooked

♦ For first attempts at finger-feeding, dice or chop small cooked vegetables such as carrot, potato, swede, turnip, butter-beans, cauliflower, cabbage – or any other vegetable or pulse from 'Purées Galore' (pp. 65–74).

♦ Make a dish that can be served in small soft pieces such as Vegetable dice (below), Butter-bean loaf (p. 130), Soya bean loaf (p. 136), Nut roast (p. 125), or Baked lentil roast (p. 128).

Vegetable dice

1 hard-boiled egg yolk or 1 tablespoon mild Cheddar cheese, grated, or 1 tablespoon almonds or other nuts, finely ground
2 tablespoons freshly cooked carrot, potato, parsnip, swede or turnip

Boil egg safely (see p. 116), and mash yolk finely. Mash vegetable(s) and add egg yolk or ground nuts or cheese. If adding cheese, make sure the vegetables are still really hot to allow it to melt. Spread evenly in a shallow rectangular dish, smoothing the top with the back of a spoon. Cut into bite-sized dice and serve.

Raw
Once your baby is chewing cooked vegetables, offer some raw.

- First, small pieces of soft vegetables such as:
  - ◇ avocado
  - ◇ tomato – washed, peeled, deseeded and with any hard core cut away
  - ◇ cucumber – washed, peeled and deseeded
  - ◇ sweet pepper – red (the sweetest), yellow or green – washed and deseeded
  - ◇ crisp lettuce – washed
- Then harder vegetables, washed, peeled, if appropriate, and finely grated or cut into sticks or chunks to chew at. Avoid small hard pieces that might cause choking and supervise constantly. Try:
  - ◇ carrot
  - ◇ cabbage
  - ◇ celery
  - ◇ courgette
  - ◇ fennel
  - ◇ parsnip
  - ◇ swede
  - ◇ turnip
  - ◇ vegetable marrow
- When teething, sticks or chunks of vegetables such as carrot, chilled for a few minutes in iced water, can be wonderfully soothing to tender gums.

FRUIT
- Dice or chop cooked fruit and well-washed soft raw fruits such as:
  - ◇ apple – cook at first, then peel, core and grate or chop
  - ◇ apricot, fresh and ripe – peel and remove stone
  - ◇ banana – slice

◇ cherries – peel at first, remove stones
◇ dried fruits, apricots, prunes, figs – cook and remove stones and seeds as appropriate
◇ grapes – peel, deseed, halve or quarter
◇ kiwi fruit – peel, deseed
◇ mango – halve, scoop out flesh and chop
◇ melon – dice
◇ orange – peel, remove pips, cut into small pieces
◇ peach – peel and remove stone
◇ pear, soft and ripe – peel and core
◇ plums, soft and ripe – peel at first, remove stones
◇ prunes – cook and remove stones
◇ seedless raisins and sultanas – soak and cook at first, and always watch for possible choking

FISH

♦ Freshly cooked white filleted fish such as cod, haddock, whiting, coley, sole, halibut or plaice, or cooked salmon. Separate into flakes and check for stray bones before offering.

♦ Canned salmon or tuna – drain and break into small pieces.

♦ Fish dishes suitable for cutting into small bite-sized pieces include Fish savoury (p. 97), Fish mousse (p. 98), and Mini fish cakes (p. 99).

MEAT

♦ Well-cooked, lean, tender pieces of meat, cut to about the size of a pea to begin with. Prepare and cook as in 'Purées Galore' (pp. 88–9).

◇ chicken
◇ turkey
◇ lamb

◇ lamb's kidney
◇ lamb's liver
◇ beef

♦ Suitable meat recipes include Liver and beef pâté (p. 108), Kidney and beef pâté (p. 110), and Pasta pick-up (opposite).

Pasta pick-up

*2–3 tablespoons freshly cooked small pasta – rings, spirals or
  macaroni*
2 tablespoons freshly cooked and diced carrot or other vegetable
*2–3 tablespoons freshly cooked lean, tender meat – lamb's liver or
  lamb's kidney – diced into small pieces*
1 tomato, washed, peeled, deseeded and chopped

Fold ingredients together. Reheat, if you wish, on a deep
plate, covered, over gently boiling water, until piping hot, 20–
30 mins.

EGGS AND CHEESE

◆ Hard boil an egg (see p. 116), and cut into small pieces – yolk
only for babies under about 8 months.

◆ Grate, or cut, mild Cheddar cheese into pea-sized pieces.

◆ Drain and crumble cottage cheese.

◆ Mix grated Cheddar cheese or crumbled cottage cheese

with apple and tomato or any other cooked or raw vegetables and fruits, prepared as suggested on pp. 65–80.

◆ Toast one side of a piece of wholemeal bread, spread the other lightly with butter or sunflower margarine and cover with Cheddar cheese, grated or thinly sliced. Pop under a medium grill until cheese melts. Cut into fingers or dice and allow cheese to cool a little.

◆ Mix mild Cheddar cheese with hot mashed potato as in Potato plus (p. 211), omit milk, and form into dice.

NUTS

◆ Mix finely ground nuts with mashed pulses or vegetables as in Vegetable dice (p. 142).

◆ Other recipes to dice include: Nut roast (p. 125), Rice and nut roast (p. 126), Soya nut savoury with the tomato purée omitted (p. 127) and Butter-bean and almond delight with the milk omitted (p. 131).

HEALTHY RUSKS AND CAKES

Rusks

½-inch (1–2 cm) thick slices wholemeal bread

Cut into neat fingers and place on a baking tray, covered by another baking tray to keep rusks smooth.

Bake at 275 °F (140 °C), Gas 1, until light brown and crisp right through, about 30 mins, turning once halfway.

Store in an airtight container for up to two weeks.

These are far healthier than bought rusks, all of which are high in sugar. They are more nutritious and much less expensive too.

Rice and apple cakes
(makes 4–6 small cakes)

*1 teaspoon sunflower seeds or sunflower (seed) spread, or 1 teaspoon
  ground almonds*
¼ eating apple
4 tablespoons cooked rice
1 teaspoon baby rice
1 dessertspoon tahini
Few drops sunflower oil

If using sunflower seeds, grind finely. Wash, peel, core and
grate apple.

Combine cooked rice with baby rice, grated apple, tahini
and ground sunflower seeds, sunflower (seed) spread or ground
almonds. Mix well. Spoon into a lightly oiled rectangular baking
dish or into individual bun tins. Level with the back of a
spoon to make cakes ¼–½ inch (1–1.5 cm) deep.

Bake at 350 °F (180 °C), Gas 4, for 20 mins.

If in one piece, cut into small squares. Allow to cool. Store
any left over in an airtight container in the refrigerator for up
to 2 days.

Banana and date cake

12 cooking dates (not sugar-rolled)
1 banana
1½ tablespoons sunflower oil
1 heaped tablespoon ground almonds
8 tablespoons Ready Brek or similar instant hot oat cereal
3 tablespoons baby rice

Remove any stones from dates and peel banana. Put them in a
liquidizer with the sunflower oil, ground almonds, Ready Brek
or similar oat cereal, and the baby rice. Whizz until thoroughly
blended – a thick dough-like mixture. Turn into a lightly oiled
baking dish about 7 × 6 inches (21 × 18 cm), to make a cake

about ½ inch (1.5 cm) deep. Level top with the back of a spoon.

Bake at 350 °F (180 °C), Gas 4, until firm and just brown on top, 20–25 mins. Allow to cool for 10 mins before turning out. Serve cut into fingers.

Store any left over in an airtight container in the refrigerator for up to 3 days.

SANDWICHES

Make first offerings postage-stamp size, with thinly sliced bread sparingly spread with butter or sunflower margarine. Use wholemeal bread whenever possible but vary it by using white, too, occasionally. With the following healthy fillings, sandwiches make nutritious meals.

Cheese

◆ Mild Cheddar, Edam, Gouda or any other mild hard cheese, thinly sliced, finely grated and beaten with a little butter or margarine, or put through a hand blender and softened with boiling water – 1 oz (25 g) cheese to 1 tablespoon water.

◆ Cottage cheese, curd cheese, or another soft white cheese (see pp. 7–8).

◆ Cheese, as above, combined with:
   ◇ thick tomato or avocado purée (pp. 73 and 65)
   ◇ apple, a smear of date, or another fruit purée (see pp. 74–80)
   ◇ finely ground nuts
   ◇ Almond and apricot spread (p. 150)
   ◇ a manufactured pure fruit spread (see p. 15)
   ◇ thickly puréed pulses as in Lentil and tomato potage (p. 134)

Egg

◆ Hard-boiled as on p. 116, mashed finely with a dot of butter or sunflower margarine and a few drops of milk.

◆ Prepared as above and combined with thickly puréed tomato (p. 73).

Fruit
◆ Try fruits such as apples, apricots, bananas, blackcurrants, raspberries, blackberries and dates – prepare as in 'Purées Galore' (pp. 74–80) and purée thickly, chop or mash.
◆ Use tomatoes in the same way; or avocados, for which no butter or margarine is necessary.
◆ Combine puréed fruits with:
  ◇ finely ground almonds or other nuts, as in Almond and apricot spread (p. 150)
  ◇ a smooth nut butter (peanut, hazelnut or cashew nut)
  ◇ tahini
  ◇ sunflower (seed) spread
  ◇ a puréed pulse, as in Fruity soya (p. 158)
  ◇ Soy spread (p. 150)
◆ Combine one fruit with another:
  ◇ banana and date
  ◇ apple and date, blackcurrant or raspberry
  ◇ apple or banana and fig
  ◇ banana and blackcurrant, blackberry or raspberry
◆ For convenience, occasionally, use a manufactured fruit spread made from real fruit with no added sugar (see p. 15), in place of puréed fresh fruit in the above combinations.

Nuts and seeds
◆ Finely ground in combination with:
  ◇ thickly puréed fruit (pp. 74–80)
  ◇ thickly puréed tomato (p. 73)
  ◇ a manufactured pure fruit spread
  ◇ a pulse purée, as in Butter-bean and almond delight (p. 131)
  ◇ Soy spread (p. 150)
◆ For convenience, use manufactured nut and seed spreads:

149

◇ a smooth nut butter (peanut, hazelnut or cashew nut)
◇ tahini
◇ sunflower (seed) spread

A FEW SPREADS

Almond and apricot spread

2 cooked apricots
3 teaspoons ground almonds
2 teaspoons apricot cooking liquid, milk or water

Mash apricots finely, stir in almonds and add sufficient cooking liquid, milk or water, to make a thickish spread.

This is delicious, nutritious and, like the other recipes in this section, naturally sweet.

Banana, almond and carob spread

1 ripe banana
2 tablespoons ground almonds
1 heaped tablespoon carob powder*

Mash banana, add ground almonds and carob powder. Mix to a smooth paste. Store any left over in a clean, airtight jar in the refrigerator for up to 24 hrs.

Soy spread

1 teaspoon butter or sunflower margarine
1 teaspoon soya flour
½ teaspoon milk or water
Flavouring – see below

* Carob powder is a naturally sweet alternative to cocoa, available at health food shops.

Cream margarine or butter, stir in flour and add sufficient milk or water, a drop at a time, to make a thick spread.

Stir in flavouring of your choice – thickly puréed fruit such as pear, raspberries, banana, dates or prunes (see 'Purées Galore', pp. 74–80); thickly puréed tomato (p. 73); ½ teaspoon tahini or sunflower (seed) spread; 1 teaspoon ground almonds or cashew nuts; 1 teaspoon smooth peanut butter; 1 teaspoon manufactured sugar-free pure fruit spread.

SCRUMPTIOUS PUDDINGS

Fresh fruit is the healthiest pudding for a baby – choose from the variety in 'Purées Galore' (pp. 74–80). But if your baby has a weakness for sweet foods, a pudding as part of a meal is much better than sweets and biscuits between meals. It means you can ensure that the ingredients are wholesome – fresh fruit, milk, eggs, ground nuts and so on. So here are a few that are particularly good.

Apple brown Betty

1 small eating apple, or piece of Bramley cooker, about 3 oz (75 g)
Few drops sunflower oil
2 tablespoons wholemeal breadcrumbs
Small nut of butter or sunflower margarine -

Wash, peel, core and thinly slice apple. Lightly oil a small casserole (avoid aluminium), and arrange apple and breadcrumbs in layers, finishing with crumbs. Spoon 3 tablespoons water over the top, dot lightly with butter or margarine and cover with lid or greaseproof paper. Bake at 350 °F (180 °C), Gas 4, or steam, until apples are tender, about 45 mins.

For babies under about 6 months, put through a hand blender.

For bigger appetites, plain yoghurt goes well with this pudding.

Apple mousse

½ hard-boiled egg yolk or 1 tablespoon finely ground cashew nuts
1 small eating apple
¼ teaspoon gelatine or agar-agar (the vegetable alternative)
Few drops lemon juice

If using, boil egg as on p. 116. Mash half of yolk and mix to a cream with a teaspoon of milk or water.

Wash, peel, core and grate the apple. Cook it with 3 table-spoons water in a small stainless steel saucepan, covered, until soft, about 5 mins. Remove from heat, sprinkle gelatine or agar-agar on to the cooked apple and stir until it is dissolved.

Mash apple and add egg cream or ground nuts, and lemon juice. Pour into a small bowl, cool quickly, then refrigerate until set, 2–3 hrs.

Apple and nut cream

1 small eating apple or piece of Bramley cooker, about 3 oz (75 g)
2 tablespoons finely ground cashew nuts or almonds
1 tablespoon milk or water
1 teaspoon plain yoghurt (optional)

Wash, peel, core and chop the apple into segments. Bring ½ inch (1.5 cm) of water to the boil in a stainless steel saucepan, add apple and simmer until tender, 3–4 mins. Drain off surplus liquid, save for a drink, and mash apple.

In a blender, whizz the ground nuts with milk or water, or beat them together, until smooth and creamy, 1–2 mins. If including, add yoghurt.

Top the apple with the nut cream or combine the two.

Baked egg custard

1 egg – yolk only for babies under about 8 months
¼ teaspoon date purée (p. 76) or honey
¼ pint (5 fl oz, 125 ml) milk
Pinch of nutmeg

Beat whole egg or yolk only, as appropriate, with date purée or honey. Add milk and mix well. Pour into a small casserole, sprinkle with nutmeg, and bake at 325 °F (160 °C), Gas 3, or steam, until firmly set, when a knife inserted will come out clean, 35–40 mins.

Eggless baked custard

2 teaspoons fine maizemeal or cornmeal
1 teaspoon soya flour
1 teaspoon tahini
½ teaspoon date purée (p. 76) or honey
⅓ pint (7 fl oz, 175 ml) milk

In a cup mix cornmeal or maizemeal with the soya flour, tahini, date purée or honey, and enough milk for a smooth paste. Bring rest of milk to the boil and stir into paste. Return to the saucepan and, over a gentle heat, stir until it simmers. Continue to cook, stirring, for 2–3 mins. Turn into a small casserole, cover with a lid and bake at 325 °F (160 °C), Gas 3, or steam, until cooked and set, 25–30 mins.

Baked rice and almonds

2 teaspoons ground almonds
1 teaspoon pudding rice
¼ pint (5 fl oz, 125 ml) milk
Pinch of nutmeg

Wash rice in a sieve and put it in a small baking dish with the ground almonds and milk. Stir to mix, sprinkle with nutmeg and bake at 225 °F (110 °C), Gas ¼, until rice is soft and top golden, 1½–2 hrs.

For babies under about 6 months, purée in a blender.

The ground almonds provide sufficient natural sweetness in this delicious rice pudding.

Banana and nut trifle

3–4 cooked apricots or an equivalent quantity of another fruit
from 'Purées Galore' (pp. 74–80), or 1 tablespoon sugar-free pure
fruit spread
1 dessertspoon ground almonds
1–2 teaspoons pure apple or orange juice
½ small banana
2–3 tablespoons Baked custard (opposite), or Custard sauce (p. 157),
or Nut cream (p. 153), or plain yoghurt or fromage frais

Mash apricots or other fruit, add ground almonds and enough juice for a soft purée. Slice banana and spread evenly over the base of a small dish, cover with the fruit and nut mixture and top with one of the custards, nut cream, yoghurt or fromage frais.

Blackcurrant yoghurt

2 tablespoons blackcurrants, fresh or frozen
¼ teaspoon apple or blackcurrant concentrate or honey
3 tablespoons plain yoghurt or fromage frais

If fresh, first wash blackcurrants and remove any stalks. Bring 4 tablespoons water to the boil, add blackcurrants with fruit concentrate or honey and simmer until soft, 5 mins, or about 15 mins if blackcurrants are frozen. Sieve, discarding seeds and skin, and stir into yoghurt or fromage frais.

Try also raspberries, blackberries, a piece of banana, or another fruit, puréed or mashed, with yoghurt. Alternatively, mash a banana in place of the yoghurt and omit the fruit concentrate or honey.

Chocolate pudding

1 egg – yolk only for babies under about 8 months
1 teaspoon date purée (p. 76) or honey
1 teaspoon cocoa powder
⅓ pint (7 fl oz, 175 ml) milk

Beat egg. Mix the date purée or honey and cocoa powder to a smooth paste with a little of the milk. Bring the rest of the milk to the boil and pour on to the paste, stirring. Pour this hot cocoa on to the beaten egg, stirring.

Turn into a small heatproof dish and bake at 325 °F (160 °C), Gas 3, or steam, covered with foil, until firmly set, when a knife inserted will come out clean, 35–40 mins.

Eggless chocolate pudding

2 teaspoons fine maizemeal or cornmeal, ground rice or semolina
2 teaspoons soya flour
1 heaped teaspoon cocoa powder
1 teaspoon date purée (p. 76) or honey
⅓ pint (7 fl oz, 175 ml) milk

Mix the maizemeal, cornmeal, ground rice or semolina with the soya flour, cocoa powder, date purée or honey and a little of the milk to make a smooth paste. Bring the rest of the milk to the boil and pour on to the paste, stirring. Return to the pan and, over a gentle heat, stir until it simmers. Continue to cook, stirring, for 2–3 mins.

Turn into a small casserole, cover with foil and bake at 325 °F (160 °C), Gas 3, or steam, until cooked and set, 25–30 mins.

Custard sauce

1 teaspoon gram flour or fine maizemeal or cornmeal
2 teaspoons soya flour
⅓ pint (7 fl oz, 175 ml) milk
¼ teaspoon date purée (p. 76) or fruit concentrate or honey
  (optional – if sweetening is required)

In a cup mix gram flour, maizemeal or cornmeal with the soya flour and a little of the milk to make a smooth paste. Bring the rest of the milk to the boil and pour on to the paste, stirring. Return to the pan, bring back to the boil, stirring, then lower heat and simmer gently, stirring frequently, until cooked, 4–5 mins.

Both gram flour and cornmeal make delicious custards and many babies will accept them as they are. If slight sweetening is required add date purée, fruit concentrate or honey to hot custard.

Fruit and nut jelly

1 teaspoon gelatine or agar-agar (the vegetable alternative)
5 tablespoons pure orange juice
2 teaspoons ground almonds
⅓ banana
3 tablespoons fruit purée from 'Purées Galore' (pp. 74–80), such as
  apple, pear or apricot

Bring water to the boil in a stainless steel saucepan, remove from heat, sprinkle on gelatine or agar-agar and stir until it dissolves. Stir in orange juice and ground almonds.
  Line a small dish or mould with the banana, sliced or mashed, arrange fruit purée on top, and pour jelly mixture over. Refrigerate until set, 4–5 hrs. Serve from dish or turn out of mould.

Fruity soya

1 tablespoon soya bean purée (p. 83)
2 tablespoons thickly puréed fruit from 'Purées Galore' (pp. 74–80),
 such as apple, blackberry, raspberry, apricot or prune
1 tablespoon diluted pure fruit juice or milk
1 tablespoon plain yoghurt (optional)

Mix soya bean purée and fruit purées together, adding enough diluted fruit juice or milk for softness, and yoghurt for a creamier texture.

Ground rice and nuts

1 teaspoon ground brown rice (or ground white rice will do)
¼ pint (5 fl oz, 125 ml) milk
2 teaspoons finely ground cashews or almonds

Mix ground rice to a paste with a little of the milk. Bring the rest of the milk to the boil and pour on to the paste gradually, stirring. Return to the pan and stir until it boils. Simmer until cooked, 5–8 mins, stirring occasionally. Stir in ground nuts.

Orange and date bread pudding

1 slice wholemeal bread, from a large loaf
2 tablespoons pure orange juice
½ egg yolk, or 1 teaspoon gram flour and 2 teaspoons soya flour
¼ teaspoon date purée (p. 76)
¼ pint (5 fl oz, 125 ml) milk

Remove crusts from bread and break remainder into pieces. Place in a small bowl, cover with the orange juice and leave to soak.

If using egg, beat the yolk and add date purée and milk.

If using gram and soya flours, mix the two to a smooth paste with the date purée and a little of the milk. Bring the rest of the milk to the boil and pour on to the paste, stirring.

Return to the pan. Bring back to the boil, stirring, lower the heat, and simmer sauce, still stirring, for 4–5 mins.

Mix orange-soaked bread with either the egg mixture, or the gram flour sauce. Turn into a lightly greased casserole (avoid aluminium), cover with lid or greaseproof paper, and bake at 350 °F (180 °C), Gas 4, or steam, until firm and, for the egg version, dry, 35–40 mins.

Orange (or Lemon) custard

1 egg yolk, or 1 teaspoon gram flour or cornmeal and 2 teaspoons
  soya flour plus 1 teaspoon tahini
¼ pint (5 fl oz, 125 ml) milk
1 tablespoon freshly squeezed orange or lemon juice
¼ teaspoon date purée (p. 76) or honey for lemon version

For egg version, make Baked egg custard (p. 154), mixing fruit juice and date purée or honey, if using, with beaten egg before adding the milk.

For flour version, follow Eggless baked custard recipe (p. 154) and add fruit juice and date purée or honey, if using, just before turning into the casserole.

Pears and carob sauce

½ ripe pear
1 heaped teaspoon carob powder (see p. 151)
1 heaped tablespoon plain yoghurt
1 dessertspoon milk

Wash, peel, core and chop or mash pear.

Sieve or press any lumps out of carob powder with a spoon and mix with yoghurt until blended. Add milk. Serve pear topped with, or stirred into, the carob sauce.

Tofu and prunes

5 cooked prunes
2 oz (50 g) tofu, drained and cubed

Remove any stones from prunes and mash them with the tofu. Alternatively, whizz together in a liquidizer until smooth.

Tofu is very nutritious, ready in an instant and soft – an ideal food for babies, once weaning begins. Replace the prunes with any acceptable fruits (see 'Purées Galore', pp. 74–80), for an easy, nourishing pud.

Tofu orange sponge

6 tablespoons pure orange juice
2 oz (50 g) tofu, cubed
1–2 tablespoons plain yoghurt or curd cheese, or another soft white cheese

This recipe is ideal for tofu that has been stored in the freezer, as it is more spongy and absorbent.

Mix the orange juice and an equal amount of water in a cup and add cubes of tofu, which should be covered by the liquid. Leave to marinate in the fridge for 3–4 hrs. Drain tofu, saving liquid, and mash with the yoghurt or cheese, adding a little of the orange marinade to soften.

Tofu cream pudding

2 oz (50 g) tofu, drained and cubed
1 tablespoon plain yoghurt
¼ teaspoon date purée (p. 76) or honey
1 teaspoon milk

Whizz tofu, yoghurt, date purée or honey, and milk in a liquidizer until creamy.

This pud is also good with fruit, or with 1 dessertspoon of ground almonds added to the mixture.

IRRESISTIBLE ICES

While some babies enjoy ices, and some find them soothing when teething, quite a few are 3 or 4 years old before they can accept their sudden coldness.

However, as most older children and many adults find them irresistible, here are a few to make from naturally sweet wholesome ingredients that we have found delicious. For practical purposes, some of the recipes are given in family quantities.

If you do not have a freezer, it is possible to use the ice-making compartment of a refrigerator. Turn it to the coldest setting half an hour before you need it and switch back to normal once the ice-cream has frozen.

For soft, creamy ices, transfer to the refrigerator half an hour or so before serving.

Apricot ice-cream

10 apricots, fresh or dried
1 dessertspoon arrowroot
1 teaspoon date purée (p. 76) or fruit concentrate or honey
  (optional – if sweetening is required)
⅓ pint (7 fl oz, 175 ml) milk
2 teaspoons sunflower oil

Prepare, cook and purée apricots as on p. 74.

Mix arrowroot and date purée, fruit concentrate or honey, if using, to a smooth paste with a little of the milk. Bring the rest of the milk to the boil and pour over the paste, stirring. Return to the pan and bring back to the boil. Reduce heat and simmer for 1 min, stirring. Remove from heat and add puréed apricots and sunflower oil. Mix well or whizz in a liquidizer.

Pour into a container and cool quickly by standing in iced water, then freeze. When almost frozen, 1–2 hrs, remove and mix well with a fork before returning to freeze solid, 3–4 hrs.

Banana, apricot and nut ice-cream

10 apricots, fresh or dried
2 ripe bananas
4 oz (100 g) cashew nuts, ground powder fine

Prepare, cook and purée apricots as on p. 74. Peel and slice bananas. Whizz apricots, bananas and ground nuts in a liquidizer until blended. Turn into a container and freeze, 3–4 hrs.

Chocolate ice-cream
(for babies over about 8 months)

1 12 oz (325 g) can evaporated milk
2 level teaspoons gelatine or agar-agar (the vegetable alternative)
3 tablespoons (1½ oz, 40 g) cocoa powder
3–5 teaspoons date purée (p. 76) or honey
1 teaspoon vanilla essence

Boil the unopened can of evaporated milk, covered with water, for 15 mins. Cool and chill in the refrigerator overnight.

Whisk chilled evaporated milk until light and fluffy.

Bring 5 tablespoons water to the boil, remove from heat. Sprinkle on the gelatine or agar-agar and stir until it dissolves. Whisk the hot jellied liquid slowly into the fluffy milk. Freeze until half frozen, 1–2 hrs.

Meanwhile, bring 3 tablespoons water to the boil, pour on to the cocoa, stirring. Add vanilla essence and enough date purée or honey to sweeten. Leave to cool.

Whisk the half-frozen milk until fluffy again and add the cooled cocoa mixture. Refreeze until firm, 3–4 hrs.

Prune ice-cream
(for babies over about 8 months)

1 12 oz (325 g) can evaporated milk
8 oz (225 g) prunes
1 dessertspoon lemon juice
1 teaspoon apple concentrate or honey

Boil unopened can of evaporated milk, covered with water, for 15 mins. Cool and chill in the refrigerator overnight.

Wash prunes, cover with plenty of cold water and soak overnight. Bring to the boil in the same water and simmer until tender, 15–20 mins. Drain, saving liquid, cool, and remove stones.

In an electric blender, whizz prunes with 2–3 tablespoons cooking liquid, the lemon juice and apple concentrate or honey. Alternatively, mash or sieve to a purée. Put into freezer until half frozen, 1–2 hrs.

Just before removing half-frozen prunes, whisk chilled evaporated milk until thick and fluffy. Then whisk half-frozen prunes until smooth and fold into the fluffy milk. Refreeze until firm.

Apricots, peaches or plums, in place of prunes, are very good too.

Orange and lemon water-ice

1 orange, unwaxed
1 lemon, unwaxed
1 teaspoon soya flour (optional)
1–1½ tablespoons apple concentrate or honey
1 teaspoon gelatine or agar-agar (the vegetable alternative)

Wash skins of orange and lemon. Remove a thin peel from each with a sharp knife, avoiding pith. Put the peel in a stainless steel saucepan with ¼ pint (5 fl oz, 125 ml) water, bring to the boil and simmer for 15 mins. Leave to cool.

Strain and discard peel.

Squeeze juice from the orange and the lemon and mix it gradually with the soya flour, if using.

Return peel liquid to the saucepan, add apple concentrate or honey and bring to the boil. Remove from heat, sprinkle on gelatine or agar-agar, and stir until it dissolves. Add juice, stir to mix and pour into a container. Set aside to cool, then freeze. When half frozen, 1–2 hrs, remove from freezer, whisk with a fork, then freeze until firm, 2–3 hrs.

Blackcurrant sorbet
(for babies over about 8 months)

4 oz (100 g) blackcurrants, fresh or frozen
½ teaspoon apple or blackcurrant concentrate
2 teaspoons gelatine or agar-agar (the
  vegetable alternative)

Prepare, cook and purée blackcurrants as on p. 75.

In a stainless steel saucepan, mix 6 tablespoons water with blackcurrant purée and fruit concentrate, and bring to the boil. Remove from the heat, sprinkle on gelatine or agar-agar, and stir briskly until it dissolves. Pour into a container and allow to cool before freezing. When half frozen, 1½–2 hrs, mash with a fork. Return to freezer until firm, 1–2 hrs.

Blackberries and raspberries make very good sorbets, too.

Iced fruit yoghurt

4 tablespoons plain yoghurt
8 tablespoons fruit purée from 'Purées Galore' (pp. 74–80), such as
  peach, plum, apple, pear, apricot, blackcurrant, blackberry or
  raspberry
1 banana

Put yoghurt in freezer until half frozen, 1–1½ hrs, and refrigerate fruit purée. Mash the banana.

Combine half-frozen yoghurt with refrigerated fruit purée and the banana. Mix well. Freeze partially, 1–1½ hrs. Whisk with a fork to break up any ice crystals that have formed and return to freezer until firm, 1–2 hrs.

MEALS TO FREEZE

If you have a freezer, it makes sense to cook in bulk food your baby enjoys and freeze it in meal-sized portions.

TIPS FOR FREEZING BABY FOOD
1. Freeze only fresh foods in good condition.

2. Cool cooked foods quickly and freeze immediately.

3. Turn freezer control to coldest setting 2–3 hrs before the food is ready to freeze and return to normal setting when food is frozen solid.

4. Pack food in suitable airtight containers, such as lidded plastic boxes, or use polythene bags with wire twists – say several small ones inside one large – for each baby food you freeze in bulk.

5. Label each item with name of food or recipe, date cooked, and storage life.

6. Always use pre-packed frozen food within the recommended storage time.

7. Except for fish, which can be cooked safely from frozen, thaw food thoroughly, preferably in the refrigerator, and try to use as soon as it is defrosted.

8. Thawed food to be served hot should be heated to boiling point, or the heat that is normally reached at the end of cooking time.

9. Never refreeze foods, once thawed.

See also 'Using a Freezer to Full Advantage', p. 31.

Carrots (and other vegetables)

2 lb (1 kg) carrots

Turn freezer control to coldest setting.

Wash, peel and slice carrots. Bring ¼ pint (5 fl oz, 125 ml) water to the boil, add carrots and simmer until tender, 25–30 mins. Drain, saving liquid. Leave sliced, or purée by mashing with a fork or liquidizing, adding some of the cooking liquid to blend.

Cool quickly by standing, covered, in cold or iced water.

Pack in ice-cube trays or in meal-sized portions in airtight containers – lidded plastic boxes or polythene bags with wire twists. Leave ½ inch (1.5 cm) head space in each. Label with name of food, date and storage life.

Freeze immediately until solid and repack carrots that have been frozen in ice-cube trays. Return freezer setting to normal.

Store up to 6 months.

Thaw in the refrigerator, then reheat until piping hot in a basin over simmering water, or add frozen to a casserole or soup, making sure it has thawed completely and boiled before serving.

Other vegetables from 'Purées Galore' (pp. 65–74) can be frozen similarly, particularly parsnip, swede, turnip, cauliflower and courgettes.

Dried beans and peas

Pulses make excellent ingredients for baby foods (see p. 80), but the time some take to cook makes it impractical to prepare in very small quantities. Here are bulk cooking and freezing directions for a few I have found particularly useful, but if you have a favourite, one can usually replace another in the recipes.

*1 lb (500 g) butter-beans, aduki beans, black-eyed beans, haricot
beans, mung beans, red kidney beans, soya beans, dried peas or
chick-peas*

Wash and pick over beans, discarding extraneous bits and any
that are blemished.

Soak by covering with plenty of cold water and leave
overnight (8–10 hrs). Alternatively, bring to the boil, covered
with plenty of water, cook for 5 mins, cover with a lid, and
leave to soak for 1 hr.

Either way, drain soaked beans in a colander and rinse
under the cold tap.

Turn freezer control to coldest setting.

Cook by covering soaked beans with plenty of fresh cold
water – 2–4 times their bulk, depending on the cooking time –
and bring to the boil. Skim off any scum and boil rapidly,
without a lid, for 10 mins. Lower heat, cover, and simmer
until soft.

Cooking time will depend on the type and quality of the pulse,
and the softness of your water – hard water prolongs cooking.

After 10 mins of fast boiling, 15 mins for red kidney beans,
allow simmering time of up to:

30–40 mins for aduki beans and mung beans

45–60 mins for black-eyed beans and haricot beans

1–2 hrs for butter-beans, red kidney beans, whole green
peas and chick-peas

3–4 hrs for soya beans.

Pressure cooking takes approximately half the time. Follow
the instructions for your cooker.

Drain, saving liquid. Leave pulses whole, mash, or liquidize,
adding some of the cooking liquid. (Use remaining liquid, if
possible, in a soup, stew or sauce.)

Cool as quickly as possible.

Pack in ice-cube trays if puréed, or in portion-sized quantities in airtight containers – lidded plastic boxes or polythene bags with wire twists – leaving ½ inch (1.5 cm) head space in each. Label with name of pulse, date and storage life.

Freeze immediately until solid and repack any frozen in ice-cube trays in airtight containers as above. Return freezer control to normal.

Store up to 6 months.

Thaw overnight in the refrigerator or at room temperature for 2–3 hrs. Add frozen to soups or casseroles at the beginning of the cooking time, making sure they defrost thoroughly and reach boiling point.

Lentils and split peas

1 lb (500 g) red split lentils, green or brown whole lentils, yellow or green split peas

Turn freezer control to coldest setting.

Wash and pick over lentils or peas, discarding extraneous bits and any that are blemished. No soaking is necessary.

Cover with plenty of cold water, twice their bulk, bring to the boil and skim off any scum. Reduce heat, cover with a lid and simmer until soft – up to 15 mins for red lentils, 30–40 mins for whole brown or green lentils and split peas.

Drain and leave whole or purée with some of the liquid. (Use remaining liquid, if possible, in a soup, stew or sauce.)

Cool, pack, freeze, store and *thaw* as for dried beans and peas, above.

Brown (or white) rice

1 lb (500 g) brown (or white) rice

Turn freezer control to coldest setting.

Wash rice in a sieve under running cold water. Bring 2⅛ pints (1 litre, 75 ml) water to the boil (1 measure of rice to two measures of water), add rice and return to a simmer. Stir once, cover with a tightly fitting lid and simmer until soft, 40–50 mins. Drain off any liquid.

Cool, pack, freeze, store and *thaw* as in dried beans and peas, pp. 168–9.

Long-grain white rice requires only 13–15 mins simmering time.

Apple (and other fruit) purée

2 lb (1 kg) cooking apples

Turn freezer control to coldest setting.

Wash, finely peel, core and cut apple into segments.

In a stainless steel saucepan, bring ½ inch (1.5 cm) water to the boil, add prepared apples, lower heat and simmer until tender, 10–15 mins. Leave as they are, mash or liquidize.

Cool, pack, freeze, store and *thaw* as for carrots (p. 167).

Other fruits, such as apricots, fresh or dried, prunes, plums, blackcurrants, blackberries, raspberries or figs, can be frozen similarly – see 'Purées Galore' for preparation, pp. 74–80.

Fish purée

2 lb (1 kg) filleted white fish

Choose filleted cod, haddock, halibut, whiting, coley, plaice or sole, fresh or frozen.

Turn freezer control to coldest setting.

Wash and dry fish, if fresh. Cook in a steamer, or in a basin, covered, over a pan of simmering water, until flakes separate easily, 10–15 mins for fresh, up to 30 mins for frozen fish.

Remove any skin and check carefully for stray bones. Flake, or purée in a liquidizer, about 8 oz (225 g) at a time, adding any cooking liquid and enough water to blend.

Cool, pack, freeze, store and *thaw* as for Lamb purée (opposite).

Fish hotpot

1 lb (500 g) carrots
1 lb (500 g) potatoes
1 14 oz (400 g) can tomatoes
2 lb (1 kg) filleted white fish

Choose fish as for Fish purée, above.

Turn freezer control to coldest setting.

Wash, peel and slice carrots thinly. Wash, peel and cube potatoes. Sieve tomatoes and juice, discarding skin and seeds.

Bring tomatoes and juice to the boil in a stainless steel saucepan, or the bottom of a double stainless steel saucepan if you have one, add carrots and potatoes and simmer, covered, until tender, 25–30 mins.

Meanwhile, if fish is fresh, wash and dry. Steam over the vegetables if possible or cook in a heatproof bowl, covered, over simmering water until flakes separate easily, 10–15 mins for fresh, up to 30 mins for frozen fish. Remove any skin, check carefully for stray bones and flake.

Combine cooked, flaked fish with the tomatoes and carrots.

Cool, pack, freeze, store and *thaw* as for Minced lamb casserole (pp. 173–4).

For babies under about 6 months, put through a hand blender before serving.

Lamb (and other meat) purée

2 lb (1 kg) lean, boneless lamb

Turn freezer control to coldest setting.

Trim fat off meat, cut into cubes, and bring to the boil just covered with water. Reduce heat and simmer, covered, until tender, about 1 hr. Drain, saving liquid.

Whizz meat, about 8 oz (225 g) at a time, in a liquidizer, adding enough of the cooking liquid to make a soft purée.

Cool quickly by returning to pan, covering with lid, and standing in cold or iced water.

Pack in meal-sized portions in ice-cube trays, or airtight containers – lidded plastic boxes or polythene bags with wire twists – leaving ½ inch (1.5 cm) space at the top for expansion. Label with name of food, date and storage life.

Freeze immediately until solid, when any frozen in ice-cube trays should be repacked in containers as above. Return freezer control to normal.

Store up to 2 months.

Thaw completely in the refrigerator and heat to boiling point before serving. Alternatively, add frozen to soup or a casserole, heating until it has completely defrosted and boiled.

To freeze chicken, turkey, beef, lamb's liver or kidney this way, see 'Purées Galore' (pp. 88–90) for preparation, cooking and puréeing, and freeze as above.

Chicken and rice casserole

1 lb (500 g) mixed vegetables: celery, sweet corn (canned, fresh or frozen), peas (fresh or frozen), broad beans (fresh or frozen) or carrot
12 oz (350 g) long-grain brown rice
12 oz (350 g) boneless and fat-free chicken – breast, leg or wing
1 heaped tablespoon grated onion for babies over about 8 months
2 tablespoons parsley, finely chopped
1¾ pints (1 litre) Baby vegetable or Baby bone stock (pp. 177–8) or water

Turn freezer control to coldest setting.

Prepare vegetables. If using celery, wash and chop into small pieces; wash, peel and slice carrot; drain and rinse liquid off canned vegetables such as corn or broad beans.

Wash rice under running cold water. Skin chicken, trim off any fat and chop into small pieces.

Put chicken into a lidded casserole with the rice and vegetables, including onion, if using, parsley and stock or water. Stir to mix and bake at 350 °F (180 °C), Gas 4, until chicken is thoroughly cooked and the vegetables and rice are tender, 1¼–1½ hrs.

Alternatively, cook in a saucepan – bring all ingredients to the boil, lower heat, cover and simmer until chicken is thoroughly cooked and the vegetables and rice are tender, 45–50 mins.

Cool, pack, freeze, store and *thaw* as for Minced lamb casserole, below, making sure the casserole reaches boiling point when reheating after thawing.

For babies under about 6 months, drain and put through a hand blender or liquidizer before serving, adding some of the cooking liquid to soften.

Minced lamb casserole
(for babies over about 8 months)

2 lb (1 kg) lean stewing lamb
3 carrots
2 parsnips
1 small swede
1 tablespoon grated onion for babies over about 8 months
4 tablespoons sunflower oil
2 tablespoons tomato purée (p. 73)
1 pint (500 ml) Baby vegetable or Baby bone stock (pp. 177–8) or water

Turn freezer control to coldest setting.

Trim away any remaining fat or sinews from the lamb and mince finely in an electric processor, or ask your butcher to do this for you.

Wash, peel and slice or dice carrots, parsnips and swede.

Heat the oil in a large stainless steel pan, add onion and sauté until soft, about 5 mins. Add the minced meat and stir gently until brown all over. Add the prepared carrots, parsnips and swede with the tomato purée and enough stock or water to cover the meat and half the vegetables. Bring to the boil and simmer, covered, until meat and vegetables are tender, 25–30 mins.

Cool quickly by standing pan in cold or iced water. Skim off any surface fat.

Pack in meal-sized portions in airtight containers such as lidded plastic boxes or waxed or foil cartons with lids, leaving ½ inch (1.5 cm) head space. Label with recipe name, date cooked and storage life.

Freeze immediately, until solid. Return freezer control to normal.

Store up to 2 months.

Thaw completely in the fridge. To heat, bring to the boil in a stainless steel saucepan, stirring frequently. Alternatively, heat in a basin over boiling water until piping hot, stirring if necessary, about 40–50 mins.

Liquidize, mash or serve as it is, with peas, green beans or cabbage.

Lamb hotpot
(for babies over about 6 months)

6 oz (150 g) each of swede, carrot and turnip
2 lb (1 kg) lean boneless lamb
2 lamb's kidneys
1 oz (25 g) butter or sunflower margarine
1 tablespoon grated onion for babies over about 8 months
¼ pint (5 fl oz, 125 ml) Baby vegetable or Baby bone stock (pp. 177–8) or water

Turn freezer control to lowest setting.

Wash, peel and dice the swede, carrot and turnip.

Trim fat from lamb and cut into small pieces. Cut away fat, skin and hard core from kidneys. Wash and dry with kitchen paper, then slice them.

Melt the butter or margarine in a large saucepan and sauté

onion until soft, 2–3 mins. Add meat and kidney and stir gently until brown all over. Add prepared vegetables and simmer, just covered with stock or water, and a lid, until meat is tender, 1–1¼ hrs.

Cool, pack, freeze, store and *thaw* as for Minced lamb casserole, pp. 173–4.

Mash or serve as it is, with a green vegetable.

Liver and tomatoes

2 lb (1 kg) lamb's liver
1 large can tomatoes (1 lb 12 oz, 780 g)

Turn freezer control to coldest setting.

Wash liver and dry with kitchen paper, cut away any veins or skin and slice. Sieve tomatoes and juice, discarding seeds and skin.

Combine sieved tomatoes, juice and liver in a stainless steel saucepan and simmer, covered, until liver has changed colour right through, 8–10 mins.

Cool, pack, freeze, store and *thaw* as for Minced lamb casserole (pp. 173–4).

For babies under about 6 months, put through a hand blender before serving.

For older babies, serve chopped with mashed potatoes and spinach or another green vegetable.

Beef loaf

1 lb (500 g) lean stewing beef
1–1½ oz (25–40 g) butter or sunflower margarine
1 dessertspoon grated onion for babies over about 8 months
2 oz (50 g) wholemeal breadcrumbs
2 eggs, beaten – yolks only for babies under about 8 months – or 2
* dessertspoons tahini mixed with 3–4 dessertspoons water*
½ pint (250 ml) Baby bone or Baby vegetable stock (pp. 177–8) or
* water*

Turn freezer control to coldest setting.

Trim any remaining fat from beef and mince in a food processor, or ask your butcher to do this for you.

In a saucepan, melt a nut of the butter or margarine, add onion and sauté until soft, 3–4 mins. Combine the minced beef, softened onion, breadcrumbs, and beaten egg or tahini paste, adding enough stock or water to give a stiff dropping consistency.

Grease a straight-sided baking dish lightly with the remaining butter or margarine and coat with the breadcrumbs. Turn meat mixture into it, cover with foil and bake at 350 °F (180 °C), Gas 4, until cooked and tender, about 1½ hrs.

Cool quickly by standing in cold or iced water. Cut into meal-sized pieces.

Pack by wrapping each piece in overlapping greaseproof paper, and put wrapped pieces in a large plastic lidded box, or a polythene bag sealed with a wire twist. Label with name of the recipe, date cooked and storage life.

Freeze immediately until solid. Return freezer control to normal.

Store up to 2 months.

Thaw completely in the fridge. Serve cold, or heat in a covered baking dish at 350 °F (180 °C), Gas 4, until piping hot, 20–30 mins. Alternatively, heat in a small basin over boiling water until piping hot, about 30 mins.

For babies under about 6 months, put through a hand blender and mix to a soft purée with a little freshly boiled milk or water.

For older babies, mash, or chop for finger-feeding, according to feeding stage reached, and serve with skinned and deseeded tomatoes or a green vegetable.

Baby bone stock

1 carrot for every half pound of bones
Beef or mutton bones fresh from a butcher, or bones or a chicken or
  turkey carcass from your own cooking

Turn freezer control to coldest setting.
  Wash, peel and slice carrot.
  Break up large bones – ask your butcher to do this with fresh bones. Simmer bones with carrot, covered with water and a lid, for 3–4 hrs.
  Cool quickly by standing pan, still covered with lid, in cold or iced water. Skim off any surface fat. Strain, discarding bones, gristle and any other solid bits.
  Pack in ice-cube trays or portion-sized containers, leaving ½ inch (1.5 cm) head space under lid. Label with name, date cooked and storage life.
  Freeze immediately until solid. If packed in ice-cube trays, remove and repack in lidded plastic boxes or strong polythene bags, sealed with wire twists. Return freezer control to normal.
  Store up to 2 months.
  Thaw completely in the refrigerator and heat to boiling point, or use the stock in a soup or casserole, making sure it defrosts completely and comes to the boil.

Baby vegetable stock

1–2 lbs (500 g–1 kg) of 3 or more vegetables such as: carrot,
  swede, turnip, celery, leeks, mushrooms, cauliflower, potato or –
  for babies over about 8 months – half an onion
½ bay-leaf
Pinch of thyme
1 dessertspoon parsley, finely chopped

Turn freezer control to coldest setting.

Wash, peel as appropriate, slice finely or chop vegetables into small pieces, and put in a stainless steel saucepan. Add boiling water to come three-quarters of the way up the vegetables. Add herbs. Bring to the boil, lower heat and simmer, covered, for 1 hr. Strain, saving stock. Save vegetables too, if you wish, for thickening soups and casseroles.

Cool stock quickly by returning to pan and standing in iced water. If vegetables are to be frozen, too, remove bay-leaf and purée before cooling.

Pack, freeze, and *thaw* stock, and vegetables if saving, as for Baby bone stock, p. 177.

Store up to 6 months.

FURTHER SUGGESTIONS

Many other recipes are adaptable for freezing – just multiply the quantities and follow freezing instructions for a similar food. These include:

From 'Nutritious Fish' (pp. 91–9)
 ◇ Fish chowder
 ◇ Fish and tomato casserole (add yoghurt or cheese just before serving)
 ◇ Fish with oats and yoghurt (add yoghurt just before serving)
 ◇ Pasta with fish and tomato (add yoghurt just before serving)
 ◇ Fish pie
 ◇ Creamed fish and cauliflower (add white cheese just before serving)
 ◇ Fish savoury
 ◇ Mini fish cakes

From 'Choice Chicken and Meat Dishes' (pp. 100–110)
- Chicken casserole
- Creamed chicken and apricots (add yoghurt just before serving)
- Chicken risotto
- Chicken and bean bake
- Irish stew
- Lamb with lentils and tomatoes
- Shepherd's pie
- Mince pudding
- Taffy's stew
- Liver mash
- Liver casserole
- Liver and beef pâté
- Liver cheese
- Kidney ragout
- Kidney and beef pâté

From 'Simple Soups' (pp. 111–115)
- Vegetable broth
- Lentil soup (add milk, if using, after defrosting)
- Chicken and celery soup
- Mini minestrone

From 'Vegetarian Fare' (pp. 120–38)
- Nut roast
- Rice and nut roast
- Baked lentil roast
- Black-eyed bean casserole
- Chick-pea hotpot
- Dilly dahl
- Haricot beans and tomatoes
- Lentil and potato savoury
- Red bean bake
- Soya bean casserole
- Soya bean loaf

From 'Finger Foods and Teatime Treats' (pp. 142–51)

◇ Vegetable dice

◇ Rice and apple cakes

◇ Sandwiches, with most fillings, but not egg – freezing makes the white leathery. Avoid also soft white cheese or other moist fillings, which could seep into and soften bread

From 'Scrumptious Puddings' (pp. 152–60)

◇ Apple brown Betty

◇ Apple mousse

◇ Orange and date bread pudding

All 'Irresistible Ices' (pp. 161–5)

ADAPTING FAMILY MEALS FOR A BABY

When your baby is ready to eat with the family, it is easier to share the same meal. With many dishes it is just a matter of taking out his portion before adding potentially harmful ingredients.

Unless otherwise stated, quantities are for two or three, as well as a baby of up to 12–18 months, around when most will be eating whatever the family is having.

FISH FOR ALL

Baked fish with cheese

4 fillets or steaks of cod or haddock, fresh or frozen
1 dessertspoon butter or sunflower margarine
2 tablespoons lemon juice
1 tablespoon soft white cheese
6 tablespoons mild Cheddar cheese, grated

If fresh, first wash fish and dry with kitchen paper.

Place fish in a shallow baking dish. Brush lightly with melted butter or margarine and lemon juice. Cover with foil and bake at 350 °F (180 °C), Gas 4, until flakes separate easily, 20–30 mins.

Baby: Remove a small piece of fish. Check carefully for stray bones, put through a hand blender, mash or flake, and mix with the soft white cheese. To heat, turn into a small baking dish, cover with foil and return to the oven, or steam until piping hot. Serve with a portion of the family's vegetables, removed before seasoning is added.

Rest of family: Sprinkle remaining fish with grated cheese and pop under a medium grill until it bubbles. Serve with a selection of vegetables, such as mashed potato, swede, carrot, peas or runner beans.

Fish Florentine

1 lb (500 g) spinach, fresh or frozen
¼ teaspoon grated nutmeg
4 fillets cod, haddock or coley, fresh or frozen
1 tablespoon soft white cheese or plain yoghurt

For the sauce:
1 tablespoon butter or sunflower margarine
2 tablespoons flour
½ pint (10 fl oz, 250 ml) milk
3 tablespoons mild Cheddar cheese, grated
Salt and pepper

If fresh, wash spinach in several changes of water to remove all grit and simmer, with last wash water adhering to the leaves, until tender, 15–20 mins. Follow instructions on pack to cook frozen spinach. Drain, add nutmeg, and whizz in a blender to purée.

If fish is fresh, first wash and dry with kitchen paper. Cook on a covered, heatproof plate over a pan of gently boiling water until flakes separate easily, 15–20 mins, or up to 30 mins for frozen fish.

Baby: Remove skin from a small piece of cooked fish and check carefully for bones. Mash or flake, and mix with a portion of the spinach and the soft white cheese or plain yoghurt. Serve with potatoes or rice – take out a portion of the family's before seasoning is added.

Rest of family: Make a sauce – melt the butter or margarine, stir in flour, cook gently for a minute. Remove from heat, stir in milk, slowly. Bring to the boil and simmer, stirring, for 2 mins. Add grated cheese, and salt and pepper to taste.

Serve fish on a bed of spinach, covered with the sauce, and accompanied by boiled potatoes or rice.

An alternative to the soft white cheese, yoghurt or cheese sauce in this recipe is the orange sauce on p. 92 – just multiply the quantities for the whole family.

Grilled plaice and baked potatoes

3–4 medium potatoes (1 for each person, including baby)
3 tablespoons plain yoghurt
1 dessertspoon mayonnaise – Hellmann's or similar
3–4 tomatoes
Peas or runner beans, frozen
3–4 plaice fillets, fresh or frozen
2–3 tablespoons sunflower oil
½ lemon
1 tablespoon herbs – parsley or fennel – finely chopped

Wash potatoes, dry with kitchen paper and score round the middle of each with a knife, lengthwise. Bake at 400 °F (200 °C), Gas 6, until tender, about 1 hr. Alternatively, wrap in kitchen paper and cook in a microwave according to manufacturer's recommendations, 8–10 mins.

Mix 2 tablespoons yoghurt with the mayonnaise and set aside to serve with the fish. Wash tomatoes and cut in half.

If fresh, first wash fish and dry with kitchen paper. Brush lightly with oil and cook under a medium grill until flakes separate easily, 3–4 mins each side for fresh plaice, about 5 mins each side if frozen. Grill tomatoes at the same time, turning once when half cooked, about 3–4 mins each side. Keep fish and tomatoes warm.

Cook peas or beans according to pack instructions, but do

not season until after your baby's portion has been removed.

Baby: Sieve half a tomato, discarding seeds and skin. Mix with 1 tablespoon yoghurt, a sprinkle of lemon juice and a pinch of parsley or fennel. Remove skin from a small piece of fish and check for stray bones. Mash or flake, and fold into or top with the tomato and yoghurt sauce and serve with soft baked potato and unseasoned peas or beans.

Rest of family: Sprinkle the fish with parsley or fennel and serve with wedges of lemon, the yoghurt sauce, grilled tomatoes, buttered baked potatoes and peas or beans.

Fish pie

1 lb (500 g) filleted white fish, freshly poached or steamed
8 tablespoons milk
1½ lb (750 g) potatoes, freshly boiled
4 oz (100 g) mild Cheddar cheese, grated
Salt and pepper
Nut of butter or sunflower margarine

Mash hot potato. Add grated cheese and about 4 tablespoons milk.

Remove any skin and stray bones from the fish. Flake it, and mix with 4 tablespoons milk.

Baby: Put portions of fish and potato into a small baking dish, fish first. Fork over top and bake, with the family's, at 350 °F (180 °C), Gas 4, for 25–30 mins, until golden on top. Mash, if necessary, before serving.

Rest of family: Season both fish and potato mixture. Spread fish on the base of a baking dish, cover with potato and fork over the top. Dot with butter or margarine and pop under a medium grill or bake at 350 °F (180 °C), Gas 4, until golden, about 5 or 30 mins respectively.

Both: Serve with carrots and/or a green vegetable.

Kedgeree

2 eggs (optional)
6 oz (170 g) long-grain rice
12 oz (350 g) filleted white fish, freshly poached or steamed
6 oz (170 g) plain yoghurt
Pinch of nutmeg
1–2 teaspoons mild curry powder
4 tablespoons mayonnaise – Hellmann's or similar
Salt and pepper
1 lemon
Few sprigs of parsley

If using, hard boil eggs safely (see p. 116). Shell, chop whites and mash yolks, keeping separate.

Wash rice. Bring ¾ pint (15 fl oz, 375 ml) water to the boil. Add rice, bring back to a simmer, cover with a lid, and simmer until tender, 13–15 mins. Drain.

Remove any skin and stray bones from the fish, and flake.

Baby: Take out 1–2 tablespoons each of fish and rice, put through a hand blender, mash, or leave as it is, depending on feeding stage reached. Mix with a dash of nutmeg, a drop or two of lemon juice, 1–2 tablespoons yoghurt and, if including, ½ teaspoon yolk, and ½ teaspoon chopped white for babies over about 8 months.

To serve cold, refrigerate until ready to serve. To heat, turn into a small casserole, cover, and bake at 350 °F (180 °C), Gas 4, or steam, until piping hot, 15–20 mins.

Rest of family: Thoroughly combine remaining fish, rice, nutmeg, curry powder, yoghurt, mayonnaise, chopped white of egg, if including, salt and pepper to taste.

Serve cold, refrigerating until you eat, or heat as for baby's, allowing 20–25 mins. Hot or cold, pile on to a serving platter or put into individual dishes, sprinkle with egg yolk, if using, and garnish with wedges of lemon and parsley.

Fish pâté

7 oz (200 g) can salmon or tuna
4 oz (100 g) cottage cheese or other soft white cheese
2 tablespoons plain yoghurt
1 dessertspoon butter or sunflower margarine
Salt and pepper

Drain fish and mash with the cheese and yoghurt, or blend in a liquidizer.

Baby: Take out a portion and serve with Rusks (p. 146).

Rest of family: Add lemon juice, butter or margarine, salt and pepper to taste, and pack the mixture into one large or individual pâté dishes. Fork over the top, refrigerate and serve with toast as an hors-d'oeuvre or as a dip with stalks of celery, raw carrot and root fennel.

Fish cakes

3–4 tomatoes
8 oz (225 g) filleted white fish, such as cod or haddock
8 oz (225 g) potatoes, freshly cooked and mashed with 1 tablespoon milk
2 teaspoons parsley, finely chopped
Pinch of nutmeg
Few drops lemon juice
Salt and pepper
1 egg white, beaten
4 tablespoons wholemeal breadcrumbs

Wash and halve tomatoes.

Steam fish or cook on a covered, heatproof plate over a pan of gently boiling water until flakes separate easily, 10–15 mins. Remove skin, check for stray bones and flake.

Baby: Put a portion of the fish through a hand blender or mash, according to feeding stage reached. Mix it with a portion of mashed potato, a sprinkle of parsley, a dash of nutmeg and a drop or two of lemon juice. Form into small cakes, brush lightly with milk, coat with crumbs and grill with the family's. Serve with grilled tomato, sieved, and some of the family's greens, removed before seasoning is added and chopped, mashed or puréed.

Rest of family: Mix the potato, fish, nutmeg, parsley and lemon juice, adding salt and pepper to taste. On a lightly floured board, form into cakes, brush with beaten egg white and coat with crumbs. Under a medium grill, cook the fish cakes until golden brown, about 5–7 mins each side, and the tomatoes, 4–5 mins each side.

Serve with spinach, peas or runner beans and grilled tomatoes.

Tuna-filled baked potatoes

3–4 medium baking potatoes (1 for each person, including baby)
6–8 oz (150–225 g) can tuna
4–6 oz (100–150 g) cottage cheese or other soft white cheese
2–3 tablespoons natural yoghurt (optional)
1 teaspoon capers (optional)
3–4 tablespoons mild Cheddar cheese, grated
5–6 leaves lettuce
3–4 tomatoes
Few sprigs parsley
Few stalks celery and other salad vegetables, as available

Wash potatoes, dry with kitchen paper and score round the middle of each with a knife, lengthwise. Bake in the oven, 400 °F (200 °C), Gas 6, until tender, about 1 hr. Alternatively, wrap in kitchen paper and cook in a microwave according to the manufacturer's recommendations, 8–10 mins.

Meanwhile, drain tuna, mash finely, and mix with the soft white cheese and yoghurt, if using. Refrigerate until potatoes are cooked.

Crush capers, if using. Wash lettuce, tomatoes, parsley and other salad vegetables.

Cut each cooked potato in half, via the incision, scoop out flesh and add to the tuna and cheese mixture. Mix well.

Baby: Put 3 or 4 tablespoons of the mixture into a separate bowl. Add freshly boiled milk to soften, if necessary. Heat, if you wish, in a lidded casserole in a medium oven, or steam, for 15–20 minutes. Serve with tomatoes, peeled, deseeded, and chopped into small pieces or puréed.

For older babies able to chew, serve the potato mixture in the jacket with pieces of well-washed salad vegetables, as well as the tomato.

Rest of family: Add crushed capers, if using, to the mixture and pile back into the potato jackets. Sprinkle with the grated Cheddar and pop under a medium grill until golden brown. Serve garnished with sprigs of parsley on a bed of lettuce and quartered tomatoes, with other salad vegetables.

MEAT TO SHARE

Braised lamb

1 onion
8 oz (225 g) potatoes
8 oz (225 g) carrots
8 oz (225 g) swede
8 oz (225 g) parsnips
4–5 stalks celery
1 lb (500 g) lean braising lamb
4 tablespoons sunflower oil
¾ pint (15 fl oz, 375 ml) Baby bone or Baby vegetable stock (pp. 177–8), or water
Salt and pepper
1 bay-leaf
2 teaspoons parsley, finely chopped
Pinch of thyme

Peel and chop onion finely. Wash, peel and slice the potatoes, carrots, swede and parsnip. Clean and chop celery. Trim any fat off the meat.

Heat the oil, sauté the onion until soft, 3–4 mins, add meat and brown lightly. Drain meat and onion and discard oil. Place vegetables in a stainless steel saucepan, then meat and onion and enough stock or water to cover vegetables. Cover and simmer gently, or bake in a casserole dish at 350 °F (180 °C), Gas 4, until the meat is tender, about 2 hrs.

Baby: Remove a piece of meat and a selection of vegetables (avoiding onion for a baby under about 8 months), and 3–4 tablespoons of the liquid. Leave to cool, then skim off any surplus fat. Put through a hand blender, mash or chop, according to feeding stage reached. Reheat, stirring, in a small saucepan.

Rest of family: Season casserole to taste, add bay-leaf, parsley and thyme. Simmer or bake for a further 15 mins.

Chicken, beef, lamb's liver or kidneys can be braised for the whole family, similarly.

Beef with prunes

8 oz (225 g) prunes
8 oz (225 g) carrots
1 onion
1–1½ lb (500–750 g) lean braising beef
4 tablespoons sunflower oil
½ pint (10 fl oz, 250 ml) Baby bone or Baby vegetable stock (pp. 177–8), or water
Salt and pepper

Wash prunes, soak overnight and remove stones either at this stage or after cooking. Prepare, cook and serve as for Braised lamb, above, placing the carrots in the bottom of the pan with the prunes and browned meat and onion on top.

Family casserole

*1 lb (500 g) bone-free stewing meat – lamb, beef, rabbit, chicken or
other fowl*

*1–1½ lb (500–750 g) mixed vegetables – carrot, plus some swede,
turnip, parsnip, celery and/or sweet corn*

*7 heaped tablespoons (8 oz, 225 g) of a pulse, canned or pre-cooked,
such as butter-beans, haricot beans or red kidney beans*

*¾ pint (15 fl oz, 375 ml) Baby bone or Baby vegetable stock (pp.
177–8), or water*

1 teaspoon salt

¼ teaspoon pepper

1 bay-leaf

3 teaspoons parsley, finely chopped

½ teaspoon marjoram, thyme or oregano

Trim any fat off meat and cut into cubes. Wash, peel and slice
vegetables as appropriate. If using a canned pulse, drain and
rinse.

Put meat, vegetables and cooked pulse into a saucepan, add
stock or water to just cover, and put on lid. Bring to the boil,
lower heat and simmer gently until the meat is tender, 1–2 hrs.

Baby: Remove a portion of meat, vegetables, pulse and,
separately, cooking liquid. Leave liquid to cool, then skim off
any surplus fat and bring to the boil. Put meat, vegetables and
pulse through a hand blender, or mash or chop according to
feeding stage reached, and moisten with a little of the cooking
liquid.

Rest of family: Add salt, pepper, bay-leaf, parsley and
other herbs to the casserole and simmer for a further 5 mins.

Both: Serve with mashed potatoes and peas, sprouts or
green beans – unseasoned for baby.

Spaghetti Bolognese
(for babies over about 8 months)

8 oz (225 g) lean beef
1 14 oz (400 g) can tomatoes
2 oz (50 g) onion
1 stalk celery
1 clove garlic
1 oz (25 g) butter or sunflower margarine
1 tablespoon concentrated tomato purée
1 bay-leaf
4 leaves fresh basil, finely chopped, or ¼ teaspoon dried basil
8 oz (225 g) wholemeal spaghetti
Salt and pepper
2–3 tablespoons Parmesan cheese, finely grated

Cut away any fat or skin and mince beef in a food processor, or ask your butcher to do this for you.

Retain juice and sieve tomatoes, discarding seeds and any skin. Peel and chop onion finely. Wash and chop celery. Peel and crush garlic.

Melt butter or margarine in a stainless steel saucepan and sauté the chopped onion and garlic until golden. Add minced beef and stir-cook over moderate heat for several minutes. Add tomato purée, sieved tomatoes and juice, bay-leaf and basil. Cover and simmer gently until meat is tender, 45 mins – longer cooking improves the sauce. Add a little water if it becomes too thick.

Meanwhile, cook spaghetti according to instructions on pack, about 8–12 mins after plunging into boiling water.

Baby: Take out small portions of sauce and spaghetti. Mix and chop or mash.

Rest of family: Season sauce and serve on a bed of spaghetti sprinkled with Parmesan cheese.

Kidneys in tomato sauce

4 oz (100 g) wholemeal macaroni
7 lambs' kidneys
1 pint (20 fl oz, 500 ml) Baby bone or Baby vegetable stock (pp. 177–8) or water
8 tablespoons tomato purée (p. 73)
2 teaspoons parsley or chives, finely chopped
1 teaspoon basil
Salt and pepper
2 tablespoons cornflour

Cook macaroni according to instructions on pack and keep warm.

Remove fat, skin and hard core from kidneys. Wash, dry, slice and simmer with the stock or water in a stainless steel saucepan, covered, until tender, 5–10 mins.

Baby: Remove slices equivalent to about 1 kidney and chop or put through a hand blender with 1–2 tablespoons cooked macaroni. Mix kidney and macaroni with 2 tablespoons tomato purée, a pinch of basil and parsley or chives, and heat gently in a small stainless steel saucepan, stirring, for a few mins.

Rest of family: Add parsley or chives, basil, the remaining tomato purée and seasoning to taste, to the stew. Blend the cornflour with a little cold water, add to stew, stirring, until the mixture thickens and boils. Simmer for a further 3 mins.

Serve kidneys and sauce on a bed of macaroni accompanied by a green vegetable.

Liver pâté

8 oz (225 g) lamb's liver
½ teaspoon gelatine or agar-agar (the vegetable alternative)
¼ teaspoon nutmeg
½ teaspoon grated onion
Salt and pepper

Wash liver and dry with kitchen paper. Cut away any veins and skin, and slice. Simmer in 6 fl oz (150 ml) water, covered, until cooked, 7–10 mins. Remove from the heat, sprinkle on the gelatine or agar-agar and stir until it dissolves. Pour into a liquidizer, add nutmeg, and whizz until smooth.

Baby: Take out a small portion. For those under about 6 months, serve as it is, or chill in the refrigerator and add a little milk to soften.

For older babies, serve sliced or diced with tomatoes, skinned and deseeded, and pieces of other salad vegetables, with peas, or with Rusks (p. 146).

Rest of family: Add onion, salt and pepper to taste and whizz liver for a few more secs. Turn into a mould, cool, and refrigerate.

Serve sliced with salad, or with toast as an hors-d'oeuvre.

Meat loaf

1 lb (500 g) lean stewing lamb or beef
4 heaped tablespoons wholemeal breadcrumbs
¼ teaspoon ground mace
2–3 teaspoons sunflower oil
1 tablespoon grated onion
¼ teaspoon mixed herbs
1 small clove of garlic, peeled and crushed (optional)
1 teaspoon salt
¼ teaspoon pepper

For the sauce (if serving hot):
3 tablespoons sunflower oil
1 small onion, peeled and finely chopped
14 oz (400 g) can tomatoes
1 tablespoon concentrated tomato purée
¼ teaspoon basil
1 bay-leaf

Trim any fat off meat and mince finely in a food processor, or ask your butcher to do this for you. Mix the minced meat with the mace and breadcrumbs.

Baby: Put 2–3 heaped tablespoons of the meat mixture into a small lightly oiled casserole dish, cover, and bake or steam with the family loaf until meat is tender, about 1 hr.

Put through a hand blender and soften with a little milk or water, or dice, according to feeding stage reached.

Rest of family: To the meat mixture add the onion, mixed herbs, garlic, if using, salt and pepper. Pack into an oiled baking dish, cover, and bake at 350 °F (180 °C), Gas 4, or steam, until meat is tender, 1–1½ hrs.

Both: Serve hot with sauce below, or for very young babies 1 or 2 tomatoes puréed (p. 73). Alternatively, serve cold with a salad – for young babies just peeled, deseeded and chopped fresh tomatoes.

Sauce: Sieve the canned tomatoes, discard skin and seeds and retain juice. In a stainless steel saucepan, sauté the onion in the oil over a medium heat until soft, 4–5 mins. Add canned tomatoes, about ½ the juice, the tomato purée, basil and bay-leaf and simmer, covered, for 30 mins, adding more juice if too thick. If too thin, continue simmering without a lid until it thickens, 10–15 mins.

Roast meat

Choose a lean piece of lamb or beef, a chicken or a turkey

Trim off any surplus fat and cook in a covered roasting dish, to avoid having to baste with fat. Delay adding seasoning or any other strong flavourings and cook thoroughly, until meat has changed colour right through and the juices are clear (see p. 39).

Baby: Carve a small, lean portion and draw 2–3 tablespoons liquid from the meat by pressing a spoon into the roast – between leg and breast in poultry. Set aside to cool. Meanwhile, put meat through a hand blender or chop it. Skim fat off cooled meat juices, bring to the boil in a small saucepan and use to moisten meat.

Rest of family: Add seasoning and other flavourings to meat and continue to cook, uncovered, until brown on top, a further 10–15 mins.

Both: Serve with potatoes – mashed or baked in their jackets for baby, not roasted – and vegetables, removing baby portions before seasoning is added.

CHEESE, EGGS AND NUTS

Cheese pudding

1 pint (20 fl oz, 500 ml) milk
3 oz (75 g) wholemeal breadcrumbs
2 eggs or 2 heaped tablespoons gram flour
4 oz (100 g) mild Cheddar cheese, grated
1 tablespoon sunflower oil
Salt and pepper to taste
½ teaspoon mixed herbs
½ teaspoon French mustard, mixed with 1 teaspoon water
1 dessertspoon parsley, finely chopped

If using eggs, first bring the milk to the boil, pour over breadcrumbs and leave to soak for a few minutes. Beat eggs – yolks only for babies under 8 months – and add with cheese to soaked breadcrumbs. Mix well.

If using gram flour, first mix it to a smooth paste with a little of the milk. Bring the rest of the milk to the boil and pour on to the paste, stirring. Return to the pan and over a gentle heat simmer to thicken, stirring, 2–3 mins. Pour on to breadcrumbs, leave to soak for a few minutes, then add cheese. Mix well.

Baby: Put a small portion of the cheese mixture into a lightly oiled casserole and bake with family pudding until firm, risen and golden, about 30 mins. For babies under about 6 months, soften with a little freshly boiled milk or water.

Rest of family: For egg version, if not already included, whisk egg whites and fold into soaked mixture. For both versions, add salt and pepper, herbs and mustard to taste. Turn into an oiled casserole, and bake at 350 °F (180 °C), Gas 4, until firm, risen and golden, 35–45 mins.

Garnish with parsley and serve with a salad.

Cheese and tomato risotto

1 14 oz (400 g) can tomatoes
8 oz (225 g) long-grain white rice
6 oz (150 g) mild Cheddar cheese, grated
1 clove garlic, peeled and crushed
¼ teaspoon basil
Salt and pepper
1 tablespoon plain yoghurt (optional for the baby portion)

Sieve tomatoes, retaining juice and discarding seeds and skins.

Put ½ pint (10 fl oz, 250 ml) water into a stainless steel saucepan, add sieved tomatoes and juice and bring to the boil. Add rice and simmer, covered, until tender, about 13 mins. Stir in grated cheese until it melts.

Baby: Remove a small portion. For babies under about 6 months, put through a hand blender. Soften with the yoghurt if you wish.

Rest of family: Add garlic, basil, salt and pepper and stir risotto over a low heat for 1 min.

Serve with a crisp salad of chopped white cabbage, celery, apple and nuts.

Eggs Florentine

1 lb (500 g) spinach, fresh or frozen
¼ teaspoon nutmeg
4 eggs, hard-boiled safely (see p. 116)
1–2 tablespoons fromage frais or similar soft white cheese
Salt and pepper

For the cheese sauce:
2 oz (50 g) butter or sunflower margarine
1½ oz (40 g) plain flour
¾ pint (15 fl oz, 375 ml) milk
4 oz (100 g) mild Cheddar cheese, grated

If fresh, wash spinach in several changes of water and simmer, with last wash water adhering to the leaves, until tender, 15–20 mins. Follow instructions on pack for frozen spinach. Drain, pressing out moisture. Return to pan, stir in nutmeg. Keep warm.

Baby: Finely mash or chop a hard-boiled egg – yolk only for those under about 8 months. Mix with a portion of spinach and the soft white cheese. Heat, if you wish, in a small covered casserole standing in simmering water for 15–20 mins.

Rest of family: Melt the butter or margarine, stir in the flour and cook gently, stirring, for 1 min. Remove from heat, add the milk, gradually. Bring to the boil, stirring, and simmer for 3 mins, stirring occasionally. Add 3 oz (75 g) grated cheese.

Season spinach to taste and spread evenly over the base of a heatproof dish. Halve the eggs, and place cut side down on the spinach, cover with the sauce and top with the remaining grated cheese. Pop under a medium grill until the cheese bubbles.

Macaroni cheese

4 oz (100 g) wholewheat macaroni
2 oz (50 g) mushrooms
1 medium onion, chopped finely, plus 1 oz (25 g) butter or sunflower margarine for cooking (optional)
3 tomatoes
1 oz (25 g) butter or sunflower margarine
1½ oz (40 g) plain flour
¾ pint (15 fl oz, 375 ml) milk
6 oz (150 g) mild Cheddar cheese, grated
½ teaspoon nutmeg
1 teaspoon mustard powder
Salt and pepper

Bring 2 pints (1 litre) water to boil, add macaroni and simmer until tender, 8–12 minutes. Drain.

Wash, peel and slice mushrooms. Bring 1 inch (3 cm) water to the boil, add mushrooms and simmer until soft, 10–15 mins. If using, sauté onion in the butter or margarine until soft, 4–5 mins.

Wash, peel, deseed and chop a tomato, for baby.

Melt the butter or margarine in a stainless steel saucepan, stir in flour, and cook gently for 2 mins, stirring. Remove from heat and stir in the milk, gradually. Bring back to the boil, stirring, then simmer until cooked, 2–3 mins. Add half the grated cheese, the cooked macaroni, mushrooms, nutmeg and, for babies over about 8 months, onion if using. Stir over a gentle heat until it just boils.

Baby: Take out a suitably sized portion, purée, mash or chop, depending on feeding stage reached. Serve with tomato.

Rest of family: Stir in mustard, onion if using and not already included, salt and pepper to taste. Turn into a lightly oiled baking dish. Sprinkle with the rest of the cheese and garnish with the two remaining tomatoes, sliced. Pop under a hot grill until bubbling and golden.

Spinach and mushroom tagliatelle

1 medium onion
1 clove garlic
2 tablespoons sunflower oil
4 oz (100 g) mushrooms
8 oz (225 g) spinach, fresh or frozen
¼ teaspoon each basil and dill
¼ teaspoon nutmeg
7 oz (175 g) cottage cheese
4 oz (100 g) wholemeal tagliatelle
Salt and pepper
2 oz (50 g) mild Cheddar cheese, grated

Peel and chop onion finely. Peel and crush the garlic. Sauté together in the oil until onion is tender, 4–5 mins. Keep warm.

Wash, peel and chop mushrooms finely. If fresh, first wash spinach well and cut into strips. Bring 1 inch (3 cm) water to the boil, add prepared fresh or frozen spinach, mushrooms, and a pinch each of the basil, dill and nutmeg. Bring back to the boil and simmer gently, covered, until tender, 10–15 mins. Drain, and whizz spinach in a liquidizer with the cottage cheese.

Preheat oven to 350 °F (180 °C), Gas 4.

Put tagliatelle into a large pan with plenty of boiling water and simmer until cooked, 10–12 mins. Drain and return to the pan, away from the heat.

Baby: Mix portions of the spinach and mushroom, the tagliatelle and, for older babies, a little of the sautéed onion and garlic. Either mash or liquidize before turning into a small casserole. Cover and bake with the family's dish until thoroughly hot, 15–20 mins.

Rest of family: To spinach mixture, add onion and garlic, additional herbs, nutmeg and seasoning to taste. Whizz to mix and combine with cooked tagliatelle. Turn into a casserole, sprinkle with grated cheese and bake until top is bubbling and golden, 20–25 mins.

In place of cottage cheese, ring the changes with 4 oz (100 g) ground almonds or other ground nuts, or 5 oz (125 g) tofu, drained and crumbled.

Pasta with tomato and nut sauce
(for babies over about 8 months)

1 14 oz (400 g) can tomatoes
1 tablespoon concentrated tomato purée
1 onion, peeled and finely chopped
2 stalks celery, washed and finely chopped
¼ teaspoon oregano
¼ teaspoon basil
1 clove garlic, peeled and crushed (optional)
4 heaped tablespoons finely ground nuts – almonds, hazelnuts, cashews or peanuts
4 oz (100 g) small wholewheat pasta – twists, rings or macaroni
1 teaspoon mild Cheddar cheese, grated, or 2 teaspoons soft white cheese
Salt and pepper
2–3 tablespoons Parmesan cheese, finely grated

Sieve tomatoes, discarding seeds and skin, and save juice.

Into a stainless steel saucepan put prepared tomatoes, tomato purée, onion, celery, oregano, basil and garlic, if using. Stir to mix and simmer gently, covered, until the sauce thickens, stirring occasionally, 25–30 mins. If too thick, add a little juice or water. If too thin, simmer without lid for a few minutes. Stir in ground nuts, bring back to a simmer and remove from heat.

Meanwhile, cook pasta according to instructions on pack. Drain.

Baby: Remove a portion of the tomato and nut mixture and stir in the Cheddar or soft white cheese. Add an equal quantity of pasta. Serve as it is or mash.

Rest of family: Add salt and pepper to taste and serve the sauce on a bed of cooked pasta sprinkled with Parmesan.

In place of ground nuts, try 6 oz (150 g) of crumbled tofu.

Quiche

For the pastry:
1 dessertspoon sunflower oil
4 oz (100 g) wholemeal flour
Pinch of salt
5 oz (50 g) butter or sunflower margarine

For the filling:
1 dessertspoon sunflower oil
3 eggs and ½ pint (10 fl oz, 250 ml) milk or 1 10 oz packet tofu
 and 4 tablespoons ground almonds
½ oz (12 g) butter or sunflower margarine
5 oz (125 g) mild Cheddar cheese, grated
1 heaped tablespoon grated onion
3 or 4 tomatoes
½ teaspoon prepared mustard
Salt and black pepper
¼ teaspoon thyme

Pastry: Lightly oil a 7–8 inch (18–20 cm approx) flan dish. Sift flour and salt, and blend with butter or margarine, using fingertips, until mixture resembles fine breadcrumbs. Make a well in the centre, add 1–2 tablespoons water, a little at a time, stirring with a fork to make a firm dough. Press into one piece and roll out on a floured board. Wrap pastry round a rolling pin and unroll to line bottom and sides of oiled flan dish. Trim to fit and prick with a fork. Refrigerate.

Filling: Beat eggs, yolks only at this stage for a baby under about 8 months, and add milk. Or, if using tofu, drain it, pat dry with kitchen paper and mash. Add grated cheese to the egg or tofu filling.

Sauté onions in the butter or margarine until soft, 4–5 mins.

Baby: Take out about 5–6 tablespoons of egg mixture, or 3–4 tablespoons of the tofu version, and for babies over about 8 months, stir in a teaspoon of the cooked onion. Turn into a small, lightly oiled casserole and sprinkle the tofu version evenly with ground almonds. Bake with filled family flan until firm and dry, 30–35 mins. Serve with peeled, deseeded tomatoes, chopped or puréed (p. 73).

Rest of family: Partially bake prepared flan case blind at 350 °F (180 °C), Gas 4, until crisp but pale, 15–20 mins.

Meanwhile, to the filling, add onions, mustard, salt and pepper, thyme and, if not already in the egg version, whisked egg whites. Turn into partially cooked flan case, top the tofu version evenly with ground almonds, and bake at 350 °F (180 °C), Gas 4, until firm and dry, 35–40 mins. Cover with foil, if necessary, to prevent pastry becoming overcooked. Garnish with a ring of finely sliced tomatoes.

Serve with a green salad.

Try this flan also with the addition of 4 oz (100 g) button mushrooms, washed and sliced – sauté and add with onions.

Lentil and cheese soup
(for babies over about 8 months)

8 oz (225 g) whole green or brown lentils
1 medium carrot
3–4 oz (75–100 g) piece turnip
1 medium onion
Pinch of thyme
Pinch of basil
2 pints (1 litre) Baby bone or Baby vegetable stock (pp. 177–8), or
  water
⅓ pint (7 fl oz, 175 ml) milk
4 oz (100 g) mild Cheddar cheese, grated
2–3 tablespoons plain yoghurt (optional)
Salt and pepper
2 tablespoons parsley, finely chopped

Wash lentils and discard any extraneous bits. Wash, peel and dice the carrot and turnip. Peel and slice the onion.

Bring lentils and prepared vegetables, with the thyme and basil, to the boil in the stock or water, lower heat and simmer until vegetables are tender and lentils soft, ¾–1 hr. Drain, saving liquid, and mash or whizz in a liquidizer with some of the cooking liquid. Add remaining liquid.

Baby: Take out 5–6 tablespoons or whatever your baby is likely to eat. Add 3 tablespoons of the milk, bring to the boil, stir in ¼ of the cheese until it dissolves, but do not reboil. Once in the baby bowl, swirl in 1–2 teaspoons plain yoghurt, if including, and serve with wholemeal Rusks (p. 146).

Rest of family: Add salt and pepper to taste, the remaining milk, and bring to the boil. Add cheese and stir until it dissolves, but do not reboil. If using, swirl in yoghurt, sprinkle with parsley and serve with croutons of toasted bread.

Vegetable and cheese casserole

½ pint (10 fl oz, 250 ml) Baby bone or Baby vegetable stock (pp.
  177–8) or water
12 oz (350 g) potatoes, washed, peeled and sliced thickly
12 oz (350 g) carrots, washed, peeled and sliced
8 oz (225 g) swede, diced
8 oz (225 g) leeks, washed well and sliced
¼–½ teaspoon mixed herbs
1 onion, grated
1 oz (25 g) butter or sunflower margarine
8 oz (225 g) mild Cheddar cheese, grated
5 tablespoons wholemeal breadcrumbs
Salt and pepper

Bring the stock or water to the boil. Add prepared potatoes, carrots, swede and leeks with ¼ teaspoon mixed herbs. Simmer, covered, until tender, 25–35 mins.

Meanwhile, sauté the onion in the butter or margarine until soft, 4–5 mins.

Baby: Remove a small selection of cooked vegetables. Liquidize or mash immediately with 1–2 oz (25–50 g) grated cheese. If this is likely to be appreciated. Top with some of the grated cheese and crumbs, and grill with the family's.

Rest of family: Add sautéed onion, more mixed herbs, if you wish, salt and pepper to the vegetables, and simmer for a further 1–2 mins. Drain, saving liquid. While still piping hot, put a layer of vegetables into a deep heatproof dish, moisten with a little cooking liquid, sprinkle with cheese. Repeat, finishing with a covering layer of cheese, and top with the breadcrumbs. Pop under a medium grill until top is bubbly and golden.

Cheesecake

For the case:

4 oz (100 g) wholemeal digestive biscuits
4 oz (100 g) ground almonds, cashews or mixed nuts
4 oz (100 g) butter or sunflower margarine, melted
1 teaspoon sunflower oil

For the filling:

2 eggs
8 oz (225 g) curd, ricotta, quark or Mascarpone soft white cheese
2 teaspoons apple concentrate or honey
2 teaspoons lemon juice
½ teaspoon vanilla essence

For the case, crush or whizz biscuits and nuts in an electric blender and mix well with the melted butter or margarine. Press evenly on to the base of a lightly oiled flan dish, about 8 inches (20 cm) in diameter.

For the filling, whizz the eggs, cheese, fruit concentrate or honey in an electric blender. Alternatively, whisk the eggs and mix thoroughly with the cheese and fruit concentrate or honey.

Baby: Take about 4–5 tablespoons of the cheese mixture, mix with a drop or two of lemon juice and turn into a small buttered casserole. Bake with the family cheesecake until firmly set, 30–35 mins.

Rest of family: Add vanilla essence and remaining lemon juice to the cheese mixture, turn on to the prepared biscuit base and bake at 325 °F (160 °C), Gas 3, until set, 35–40 mins.

Both: Top with any available fruit, puréed or chopped – puréed blackcurrants, blackberries or raspberries or chopped ripe pear or peach are particularly good (see 'Purées Galore', pp. 74–80).

Tofu cheesecake

For the case:

2 oz (50 g) wholemeal digestive biscuits
2 oz (50 g) ground almonds, cashews or mixed nuts
2 oz (50 g) butter or sunflower margarine
1 teaspoon sunflower oil

For the filling:

4 oz (100 g) tofu
4 oz (100 g) curd, ricotta, quark or Mascarpone soft white cheese
Juice of ½ lemon plus finely grated rind of whole unwaxed lemon
1½ teaspoons gelatine or agar-agar (the vegetable alternative)
1–2 teaspoons apple concentrate or honey
Few drops vanilla essence

For the case, crush or whizz biscuits and nuts in an electric blender and mix well with the melted butter or margarine. Press evenly on to the base of a lightly oiled flan dish, about 7 inches (18 cm) in diameter.

For filling, drain tofu and put into an electric blender with the soft white cheese. Squeeze the half lemon, and make up to ⅛ pint (2½ fl oz, 65 ml) with water. Bring to the boil in a small stainless steel saucepan, remove from heat, sprinkle on gelatine or agar-agar and stir until it dissolves. Add the jelly liquid to the mixture in the blender, whizz to mix, then add just enough apple concentrate or honey to sweeten.

Baby: Put a small portion of the mixture, 3–4 tablespoons, into a dish and refrigerate to set.

Rest of family, including older babies: Add vanilla essence and lemon rind to the mixture, whizz to mix, turn into prepared case and refrigerate to set.

Both: Top with fruit as for Cheesecake (p. 205).

If tofu is not available, use 8 oz (225 g) of the soft white cheese.

QUICK MEALS

To produce a meal speedily for a hungry baby you need to have the right ingredients to hand. 'Quick Meals' are based on foods that require little, if any, preparation. Keep some by you, in case . . .

INGREDIENTS USED IN THE RECIPES

Fruit
♦ fresh ripe pears, apples, bananas, plums, oranges, clementines, mandarins and peaches
♦ dried apricots or prunes – soaked, cooked and possibly frozen, ready for use
♦ dates for date purée (p. 76), to sweeten when necessary

Vegetables
♦ avocados, tomatoes and cooked beetroot
♦ potatoes
♦ cauliflower, cabbage, leeks, celery and mushrooms
♦ frozen peas, broad beans, runner or French beans, sweet corn and mini portions of spinach
♦ canned tomatoes, broad beans and sweet corn

Pulses
♦ canned baked beans, butter-beans, haricot beans, cannellini beans, red kidney beans and chick-peas or other pulses, pre-cooked and frozen ready for use (see pp. 167–8)
♦ lentils, particularly split red lentils

Cheese
♦ cottage cheese, curd cheese and similar soft white cheeses (see pp. 7–8)

◆ mild Cheddar cheese
Plain yoghurt (see p. 8)
Canned tuna and salmon
Cereals
◆ baby rice and other baby cereals (see pp. 11–12)
◆ rice pre-cooked and frozen (see pp. 169–70)
◆ Ready Brek or similar instant hot oat cereals (see p. 13)
◆ flaked rice (see p. 85)
◆ Weetabix, Shredded Wheat, Ryvita, puffed rice cakes, wholewheat bread or oatcakes
Small pasta such as rings and spirals, preferably wholewheat
Nuts
◆ ground almonds and other packaged finely ground nuts
◆ whole nuts – hazelnuts, cashews, almonds, Brazil nuts, pine nuts or peanuts – ground finely
◆ peanut and other nut butters – smooth, not crunchy, to avoid the possibility of choking on nut bits
Seeds (see p. 20)
◆ sunflower seeds, finely ground
◆ sesame seeds
◆ sunflower (seed) spread
◆ tahini
Tofu (see p. 16)
Soya flour (see p. 16)

OTHER QUICK-TO-PREPARE FOODS
Eggs (see pp. 116–19)
White fish, fresh and frozen (see pp. 91–9)
Liver, fresh or frozen (see pp. 106–109)

See also 'Convenience Foods', pp. 12–16.

◆ ◆ ◆ ◆ ◆ ◆ ◆ ◆ ◆ ◆ ◆ ◆ ◆ ◆ ◆ ◆

Pasta pronto

1 canned tomato plus 8 tablespoons juice from the can
1 oz (25 g) small wholewheat pasta – twists or rings
1–2 tablespoons plain yoghurt

Sieve tomato, discarding seeds and any skin.

In a stainless steel saucepan, bring sieved tomato and juice to the boil, add pasta and simmer gently, covered, until soft, 8–12 mins, or see instructions on pasta pack for timing. Add yoghurt and stir until it just boils. To purée for very young babies, whizz in a blender.

Alternatives to yoghurt:
♦ curd cheese, fromage frais or similar soft white cheese
Optional additions:
♦ 1–2 teaspoons finely ground nuts such as almonds or cashews
♦ 1 dessertspoon mild Cheddar cheese, grated
♦ 3 mini portions of frozen spinach – add to boiling juice with pasta

Beans and tomato with cheese

1 medium tomato, fresh or canned
2 tablespoons butter-beans, pre-cooked or canned
1 tablespoon curd cheese

If fresh, first cover the tomato with boiling water and leave for 2 mins. Drain, peel and deseed. Sieve tomato, fresh or canned, retaining all juice.

If butter-beans are canned, first drain and rinse. Mash, adding tomato and curd cheese. Serve cold, or heat on a covered, heatproof plate over simmering water for 10–15 mins.

Alternatives to butter-beans:
♦ cooked or canned haricot, black-eyed, aduki, mung, cannellini, soya or red kidney beans

- cooked or canned chick-peas, dried peas, or lentils

Alternatives to curd cheese:
- other soft white cheese
- plain yoghurt

Alternatives to tomato:
- 3–4 mini portions frozen spinach, stirred over a gentle heat with a nut of butter or sunflower margarine until thawed, then cooked for 3–4 mins
- ¼ of an avocado, mashed
- ¼ of an apple or ripe pear, grated, mashed or scraped with a knife to a purée

Optional additions:
- 2 teaspoons finely ground nuts
- 1 teaspoon smooth peanut butter, tahini or sunflower (seed) spread
- 1 teaspoon soya flour
- 2 teaspoons canned tuna or salmon, drained and flaked or mashed

Fast fish

1 tablespoon (1 oz, 25 g) canned tuna or salmon
2 tablespoons plain yoghurt

Drain tuna, mash, and mix with the yoghurt, or whizz together in a liquidizer. Serve cold.

Alternatives to yoghurt:
- cottage cheese, curd cheese or similar plus 1–2 tablespoons milk

Optional additions:
- 1 tomato, peeled, deseeded and chopped or thickly puréed (save surplus juice and serve as a drink)
- ½–1 oatcake, rice cake or Ryvita, softened with 3–5 tablespoons freshly boiled milk or water
- 2–3 mini portions frozen spinach, stirred over a gentle heat with a nut of butter or sunflower margarine until thawed, then

cooked for 3–4 mins
◆ 2 tablespoons cooked brown wholegrain or white rice

Potato plus

1 small potato
1 tablespoon mild Cheddar cheese, grated
2–3 tablespoons milk

Wash potato and put into 1 inch (3 cm) boiling water. Simmer, covered, until cooked, about 20 mins. Drain, peel, mash and, while still hot, add cheese, then milk to soften.

Alternatives to Cheddar cheese:
◆ 1 tablespoon cottage cheese, curd cheese, fromage frais or similar
◆ 1 tablespoon plain yoghurt, and use less milk
◆ 1 tablespoon almonds or other nuts, finely ground
◆ 1 dessertspoon canned tuna or salmon, drained and mashed
◆ 1–2 teaspoons smooth peanut butter or tahini
◆ 2–3 mini portions frozen spinach, stirred over a gentle heat with a nut of butter or sunflower margarine until thawed, then cooked for 3–4 mins
◆ combinations of some of the above, such as ground almonds and cheese or spinach, or spinach and cheese, are also delicious with potato

Optional additions:
◆ 1 tomato, peeled, deseeded, chopped or puréed, with juice
◆ 1 dessertspoon canned sweet corn, drained, rinsed and pressed through a sieve
◆ 1–2 teaspoons soya flour, for added nourishment rather than flavour

Tasty tofu

2 oz (50 g) tofu, drained and dried with kitchen paper
1 tablespoon plain yoghurt
1 tablespoon milk

Whizz all 3 ingredients in a blender, or mash together until smooth. Serve cold, or heat in a small covered casserole, standing in or over simmering water, or bake at 350 °F (180 °C), Gas 4, for 15 mins.

Alternatives to yoghurt:

◆ fromage frais, curd cheese or similar

Optional additions for a savoury meal:

◆ 1 tomato, peeled, deseeded and chopped or puréed
◆ 2–3 mini portions of frozen spinach, stirred over a gentle heat with a small nut of butter or sunflower margarine until thawed, then cooked for 3–4 mins
◆ 1 dessertspoon canned tuna or salmon, drained and mashed
◆ ½ small freshly cooked potato or carrot
◆ 1 dessertspoon nuts, finely ground
◆ 1–2 tablespoons cooked rice or lentils

Optional additions for a fruit meal:

◆ 3–4 cooked apricots or prunes
◆ 1 ripe peach
◆ ¼ of a ripe pear or eating apple
◆ piece of banana
◆ ¼ of an orange, puréed

Tomato and cheese

1 tomato, fresh or canned
2–3 teaspoons Ready Brek or similar instant hot oat cereal
2 tablespoons fromage frais, cottage cheese, curd cheese or similar

If fresh, first cover tomato with boiling water and leave for 2 mins. Peel, deseed and quarter, retaining all the juice. Chop and sieve, or put through a hand blender. If canned, sieve tomato, retaining juice.

In a stainless steel saucepan, bring puréed tomato and juice to the boil. Pour over instant oat cereal, stir until smooth, add cheese.

Alternatives to instant oat cereal:

- a crumbled oatcake, Ryvita, rice cake, or ½ slice of wholemeal bread
- 2 tablespoons cooked rice or lentils
- 2 tablespoons baby rice or other baby cereal

Optional additions:

- 1–2 teaspoons finely ground nuts or sunflower seeds
- 1 teaspoon smooth peanut butter or another nut butter, tahini or sunflower (seed) spread
- 1–2 tablespoons small pasta cooked according to instructions on pack
- ¼ of an avocado, mashed
- 1–2 teaspoons soya flour
- 1–2 oz (25–50 g) tofu
- ¼ of an eating apple or ripe pear, puréed

Quick cauliflower cheese

3–4 sprigs cauliflower
3 tablespoons fromage frais

Wash cauliflower, put into 1 inch (3 cm) boiling water and simmer, covered, until tender, 7–10 mins. Drain, saving liquid. Chop, mash or liquidize, adding the cheese and enough cooking liquid to soften. Return to the pan and, over a gentle heat, stir until it just boils.

Alternatives to fromage frais:
♦ curd cheese or similar
Optional additions:
♦ 2 teaspoons nuts, finely ground
♦ 1 tablespoon frozen peas – cook with cauliflower
♦ 1 tablespoon cooked lentils
♦ 1 dessertspoon mild Cheddar cheese, grated – add during final heating or sprinkle on finished dish and grill until golden
♦ 1 dessertspoon Ready Brek or similar instant hot oat cereal, or baby cereal, and add an extra 2–3 tablespoons cooking liquid or milk during final heating

Black-eyed beans and yoghurt

4 tablespoons black-eyed beans, canned or pre-cooked
2 tablespoons plain yoghurt

If canned, first drain and rinse beans. Mash or liquidize and add yoghurt.

Alternatives to black-eyed beans:
♦ haricot, cannellini, soya, aduki, mung, butter-beans or red kidney beans, pre-cooked or canned
♦ chick-peas, whole or split peas, pre-cooked or canned
♦ cooked lentils
Alternatives to yoghurt:
♦ cottage cheese, curd cheese or similar

Optional additions:
- 1–2 teaspoons smooth peanut butter, tahini or sunflower (seed) spread
- 1–2 teaspoons soya flour
- 1 tomato, peeled, deseeded and chopped or puréed
- ½ an eating apple, washed, peeled and grated or puréed
- 1 tablespoon mild Cheddar cheese, grated and softened in 1 tablespoon boiling water
- 1 dessertspoon nuts, finely ground
- 1–2 teaspoons sesame seeds
- 1 dessertspoon canned tuna or salmon, drained and mashed

Almond and oat lunch

1 oatcake
3 tablespoons milk or water, freshly boiled
1 tablespoon ground almonds

Crumble oatcake and soften with the freshly boiled milk or water. Add nuts. Really good on its own, but see below for bigger appetites.

Alternatives to oatcake:
- 1 Ryvita or rice cake
- ½ slice wholemeal bread, crusts removed
- 1 Shredded Wheat or Weetabix whizzed to fine crumbs in a blender

Alternatives to almonds:
- peanuts, hazelnuts, cashews or Brazil nuts, finely ground
- sunflower seeds, finely ground

Optional additions:
- 1 tomato, fresh or canned, peeled, deseeded and puréed
- 3–4 apricots or prunes, cooked
- fresh fruit, such as ½ ripe pear or apple, a peach, or a piece of banana, mashed
- ¼ of an avocado, mashed

Easy avocado

½ ripe avocado

Choose a fruit that yields to gentle pressure. The flesh should be soft, and creamy in colour.

Cut in half, scoop out flesh, mash and serve. This is a nutritious meal on its own for a young baby – for bigger appetites, see below.

If not using immediately, leave stone in other half, sprinkle with lemon juice and refrigerate for up to 24 hrs.

Optional additions:

- 1 tablespoon cottage cheese, curd cheese or similar
- 1 tablespoon plain yoghurt
- 1 tablespoon mild Cheddar cheese, grated – soften in 1 tablespoon boiling water
- 1 tablespoon almonds or other nuts, finely ground
- 1–2 teaspoons smooth peanut butter, or another nut butter
- ½ an eating apple or ripe pear, washed, peeled, cored and grated or puréed
- 2–3 cooked apricots
- 1 tablespoon canned tuna or salmon, drained and mashed

Baked bean quickie

½ slice wholemeal bread from a large loaf
1–2 tablespoons freshly boiled milk or water
1 tablespoon mild Cheddar cheese, finely grated
1 tablespoon canned baked beans

Remove crusts from bread and crumble into a small bowl. Cover with 1 tablespoon boiling milk or water and add grated cheese, stirring.

Drain baked beans, rinse under cold tap, mash, and combine with the bread mixture. Add more milk or water for a softer consistency.

Alternatives to bread:

- 1 crumbled oatcake, Ryvita, rice cake, Weetabix or Shredded Wheat

Alternatives to Cheddar cheese:
♦ cottage cheese, curd cheese or similar

Quick kedgeree

1 tablespoon canned tuna or salmon
2 tablespoons cooked brown wholegrain (or white) rice
2 tablespoons plain yoghurt

Drain tuna or salmon and flake or mash finely. Add cooked rice and yoghurt. Mix with a fork or whizz in a blender.

Serve cold, or heat in a small covered casserole, standing in simmering water for 15–20 mins.

Alternatives to yoghurt:
♦ cottage cheese, curd cheese or similar, plus 1–2 tablespoons milk

Fish sauce with pasta

1 oz (25 g) small pasta – twists, rings or macaroni
1 tablespoon canned tuna or salmon
1 tomato, fresh or canned
1 teaspoon tomato purée (p. 73)

Cook pasta according to instructions on pack. Drain tuna or salmon, and flake or mash.

If fresh, first cover tomato with boiling water and leave for 2 mins. Peel, quarter, deseed and chop, retaining all the juice. Sieve canned tomato, discarding seeds and skin.

Into a stainless steel saucepan, put tomato with juice and tomato purée, with 1–2 tablespoons water, if necessary, to make a thickish sauce. Bring to the boil, stirring. Add fish and pasta and bring back to the boil. Liquidize for very young babies.

Alternatives to tomato purée:
◆ 1 dessertspoon plain yoghurt or soft white cheese
Optional addition:
◆ 1 dessertspoon mild Cheddar cheese, grated

Almond rice

1 tablespoon flaked rice
¼ pint (5 fl oz, 125 ml) milk
2 teaspoons ground almonds

Bring flaked rice and milk to the boil, stirring. Reduce heat and simmer, covered, stirring occasionally until cooked, about 10 mins. Stir in ground almonds and serve.
Alternatives to almonds:
◆ other nuts – hazelnuts, cashews, peanuts, pine nuts or Brazil nuts – finely ground
◆ 1–2 teaspoons smooth peanut butter or another nut butter
◆ 1 teaspoon tahini or sunflower (seed) spread
Optional additions:
◆ ¼ of an eating apple or ripe pear, finely grated or puréed
◆ 2–3 cooked apricots or prunes
◆ piece of ripe banana
◆ 2–3 teaspoons plain yoghurt or soft white cheese

Creamed cabbage

2–3 medium leaves (1 oz, 25 g) hard white, red or green cabbage
4 tablespoons milk

Wash and shred cabbage. Bring milk to the boil, add cabbage and simmer gently, covered, until tender, 6–8 mins. Whizz, with cooking liquid, in a blender.
Optional additions:
◆ 1 tablespoon finely ground nuts
◆ ¼ of an eating apple, washed, peeled, cored and chopped
◆ ½ a small, cooked beetroot

◆ 1 tomato, peeled, deseeded and puréed
◆ 1 dessertspoon cottage cheese, curd cheese, or similar
◆ 1 dessertspoon plain yoghurt
◆ 1 teaspoon smooth peanut butter or another nut butter
◆ 1 teaspoon tahini or sunflower (seed) spread
◆ 1 teaspoon soya flour
◆ 1 teaspoon mild Cheddar cheese, grated – whizz with the hot cabbage

Beetroot bonanza

4 oz (100 g) cooked beetroot
2 tablespoons milk

Slip skin off beetroot with fingers or a knife, cut off stalk end and chop into small pieces.

Bring milk and beetroot to the boil, pour into a liquidizer and whizz until blended.

Optional additions:
◆ 2 teaspoons fromage frais, cottage cheese, curd cheese or similar
◆ 2 teaspoons plain yoghurt
◆ 2 teaspoons finely ground almonds, peanuts, cashews or hazelnuts
◆ 2 teaspoons finely ground sunflower seeds
◆ ¼ of an eating apple, a Bramley cooker or a ripe pear – wash, peel, core and bring to the boil with the beetroot
◆ 1–2 tablespoons cooked rice
◆ 1–2 dessertspoons mild Cheddar cheese, grated – add to hot beetroot before blending

Mushroom, cheese and almonds

1 medium mushroom
1 tablespoon cottage cheese, curd cheese or similar
2 teaspoons ground almonds

Wash, peel and slice the mushroom. Bring 4 tablespoons water to the boil, add prepared mushroom and simmer until soft, 10–15 mins. Pour mushroom and cooking liquid into an electric blender, add cheese and almonds and whizz to a purée. Serve.

Alternatives to white cheese:
- 1 tablespoon mild Cheddar cheese, grated
- 1 tablespoon plain yoghurt

Alternatives to almonds:
- other nuts – hazelnuts, cashews, peanuts or Brazil nuts – finely ground
- finely ground sunflower seeds or pumpkin seeds
- 1–2 teaspoons peanut butter, another nut butter, tahini or sunflower (seed) spread

Optional additions:
- ½ stalk celery, cleaned and chopped into small pieces or grated, and cooked with the mushroom
- 1 tomato, peeled, deseeded and chopped (save any juice for a drink)
- 1 oz (25 g) small pasta, cooked according to instructions on pack
- 2–3 mini portions frozen spinach, stirred over a gentle heat with a small nut of butter or sunflower margarine until thawed, then cook for 3–4 mins
- 1–2 tablespoons cooked rice
- 1–2 teaspoons soya flour

Peas with tomato and nuts

1 sprig parsley (optional)
4 tablespoons peas, fresh or frozen
1 tablespoon almonds or other nuts, finely ground
2 tablespoons tomato juice or 1 tomato, peeled and deseeded

Wash parsley and shake dry.

For babies over about 10 months, serve peas raw. Otherwise, put peas into 1 inch (3 cm) boiling water and simmer, covered, until tender, 8–10 mins for fresh peas, about 3 mins for frozen ones. Drain.

Put peas with ground nuts, parsley and tomato or juice into an electric blender and whizz until smooth.

Alternative to ground nuts:
♦ 2 teaspoons smooth peanut butter or another nut butter

Optional addition:
♦ 1–2 tablespoons cottage cheese, curd cheese or similar

Sweet corn and cheese

3 tablespoons canned sweet corn
1–2 tablespoons cottage cheese, curd cheese, fromage frais or similar
1–2 tablespoons milk or water

Drain sweet corn, rinse, and whizz with the cheese in a blender, adding milk or water to soften if necessary. Serve cold or heat gently, stirring, without boiling.

Alternatives to white cheese:
♦ 1 tablespoon plain yoghurt
♦ 1 tablespoon grated mild Cheddar cheese, softened with 1–2 tablespoons freshly boiled water or milk

Optional additions:
♦ ¼ of a red or green sweet pepper, washed, deseeded and chopped
♦ 1 tomato, peeled, deseeded and chopped, with juice
♦ 1–2 teaspoons sesame seeds
♦ 1 dessertspoon finely ground sunflower seeds
♦ 1 dessertspoon finely ground nuts
♦ 1 dessertspoon canned tuna or salmon, drained and mashed
♦ 1–2 teaspoons smooth peanut butter or another nut butter
♦ 1–2 teaspoons tahini or sunflower (seed) spread
♦ 1–2 teaspoons soya flour

Banana and sweet corn custard

3–4 tablespoons sweet corn, canned or frozen
1–2 tablespoons milk
¼ banana

If using frozen corn, put 1 inch (3 cm) boiling water and simmer, covered, until tender, 3–4 mins. Drain, saving liquid. If using canned corn, drain and rinse under the cold tap.

Sieve corn, discarding skins, and add milk for a soft purée. Mash banana and add to custard.

Butter-beans and apricots

4 tablespoons butter-beans, pre-cooked or canned
6–8 apricots, cooked

If using canned butter-beans, first drain and rinse.

Mash beans with apricots, adding enough juice or water for a soft purée.

Alternatives to apricots:

- 6–8 prunes
- 1 ripe peach
- ½ a ripe pear
- piece of ripe banana
- ¼ of an orange, puréed

Optional additions:

- 1–2 tablespoons plain yoghurt
- 1–2 tablespoons cottage cheese, curd cheese or similar
- 2 teaspoons finely ground nuts
- 1–2 teaspoons soya flour
- 1–2 teaspoons peanut butter, tahini or sunflower (seed) spread

Speedy spinach

3–4 mini portions frozen spinach
Small nut of butter or sunflower margarine
1 tablespoon mild Cheddar cheese, grated
2 tablespoons plain yoghurt
Pinch of dill or nutmeg (optional)

Thaw spinach with the butter or margarine in a saucepan over a medium heat, stirring frequently, then cook for 3–4 mins. Remove from heat and add cheese, yoghurt, and dill or nutmeg, if using.

Alternatives to Cheddar cheese and yoghurt:
◆ cottage cheese, curd cheese or similar

Optional additions:
◆ 1–2 teaspoons soya flour
◆ 1–2 teaspoons almonds or other nuts, finely ground
◆ 2 tablespoons cooked rice
◆ 2 tablespoons cooked red, green or brown lentils

Banana brunch

1 ripe banana
1 tablespoon ground almonds
2 tablespoons plain yoghurt

Mash banana and mix with almonds and yoghurt.

Alternatives to yoghurt:
◆ cottage cheese, curd cheese or similar

Optional additions:
◆ 1–2 teaspoons smooth peanut butter or other nut butter, tahini, or sunflower (seed) spread
◆ 1–2 teaspoons soya flour
◆ 1 oz (25 g) tofu, drained and patted dry with kitchen paper, mashed
◆ ¼ of an apple or ripe pear, puréed
◆ 1 small ripe peach or nectarine, mashed
◆ 2–3 cooked apricots or prunes, mashed

Cheese fool

2 tablespoons cottage cheese
½ ripe pear
Few drops lemon juice

Wash, peel, core and mash pear. Sprinkle with lemon juice and mix with the cheese.

Alternatives to cottage cheese:

◆ curd cheese, fromage frais or similar
◆ 2 tablespoons plain yoghurt
◆ 2 tablespoons grated mild Cheddar cheese, softened with 1–2 tablespoons freshly boiled water
◆ 1–2 oz (25–50 g) tofu, drained and mashed, or liquidized with the pear

Optional additions:

◆ 1–2 teaspoons smooth peanut butter or another nut butter, tahini or sunflower (seed) spread
◆ 1 dessertspoon finely ground nuts
◆ 1 tomato, peeled, deseeded and chopped or puréed
◆ 2–3 cooked apricots or prunes, mashed
◆ 1–2 teaspoons soya flour

Savoury rice

1 tablespoon flaked rice or 2 heaped tablespoons baby rice
¼ pint (5 fl oz, 125 ml) milk
1 tablespoon mild Cheddar cheese, grated

If using flaked rice, add the milk and bring to the boil, stirring. Reduce heat and simmer, covered, stirring occasionally, until cooked, about 10 mins. Add grated cheese and serve.

If using baby rice, bring milk to the boil, allow it to cool a little, and stir into rice (or follow instructions on pack). Stir in cheese and serve.

Alternatives to Cheddar cheese:
◆ cottage cheese, curd cheese or similar
◆ 1–2 tablespoons pre-cooked or canned haricot beans, or another pulse, mashed

Optional additions:
◆ 1 tomato, peeled, deseeded and chopped or puréed, with juice
◆ 1 tablespoon plain yoghurt
◆ 2 tablespoons of any favourite vegetable, prepared and chopped or puréed as in 'Purées Galore' (pp. 65–74)

Soya lunch

1 tablespoon soya flour
1 medium tomato, fresh or canned

If using fresh tomato, first cover with boiling water and leave for 2 mins. Peel and deseed, retaining juice with the flesh.

Sieve tomato and mix to a smooth purée with the soya flour. Don't give up on this easy and very nutritious meal if it is not accepted first time. Try the alternatives or some of the optional additions.

Alternatives to tomato:
◆ 3–4 cooked apricots or prunes, mashed
◆ ½ a ripe pear, puréed
◆ 1 kiwi fruit, peeled and deseeded
◆ piece of banana, mashed
◆ 1 clementine, puréed

Optional additions:
◆ 1 teaspoon smooth peanut butter or another nut butter, tahini or sunflower (seed) spread
◆ 1 tablespoon plain yoghurt
◆ 1 dessertspoon finely ground nuts

Broad beano

2 tablespoons broad beans, frozen or canned
2–3 tablespoons milk
1 tablespoon plain yoghurt
1 tablespoon ground almonds

If frozen, put beans into 1 inch (3 cm) boiling water and simmer until tender, 3–4 mins. Drain. For canned beans, drain and rinse under cold tap.

Whizz beans, milk, yoghurt and ground almonds in a liquidizer until smooth.

Alternatives to broad beans:

◆ frozen peas
◆ pre-cooked or canned haricot beans, or another pulse

Alternatives to yoghurt:

◆ cottage cheese, curd cheese or similar

Creamy nut whip

1 teaspoon smooth peanut butter or another nut butter
3 tablespoons fromage frais

Whip together until soft and creamy.

Alternatives to nut butter:

◆ tahini or sunflower (seed) spread

Alternatives to fromage frais:

◆ other soft white cheeses adding a little milk to soften, if necessary

Optional additions:

◆ 1–2 teaspoons freshly squeezed orange juice
◆ ⅓ of a banana
◆ ¼ teaspoon date purée (p. 76)

FURTHER READING

If you want to know more about safe and healthy foods – for adults as well as babies – these titles are useful:

Edwards, D. and Bazalgette, P. *BBC Food Check*, BBC Books, 1989.
A practical guide to which foods are safe for the whole family to buy, cook and eat.

Lacey, Richard. *Safe Shopping, Safe Cooking, Safe Eating*, Penguin Books, 1989.
Simple rules that can protect you and your family from salmonella, listeria and other forms of food poisoning, from leading microbiologist.

Lacey, Richard. *Unfit for Human Consumption*, Souvenir Press, 1991.
An update on foods to avoid, from the same authority.

Lobstein, Tim. *Children's Food: The Good, The Bad and The Useless*, Unwin Hyman, 1988.
Highlights the risks and dangers of manufactured foods, including baby foods and additives, with advice on how to make a fuss about foods you are unhappy or dissatisfied with.

Taylor, Joan and Derek (eds). *Safe Food Handbook*, Parents for Safe Food in Association with the London Food Commission, Ebury Press, 1990.
Discusses the safety of food in detail. An intelligent approach to protecting everyone, including babies, from food hazards.

FOOD GUIDANCE INDEX

FOOD GUIDANCE INDEX

FOOD GUIDANCE INDEX

INDEX TO RECIPES

FOR THE BEST IN PAPERBACKS, LOOK FOR THE 🐧

In every corner of the world, on every subject under the sun, Penguin represents quality and variety – the very best in publishing today.

For complete information about books available from Penguin – including Puffins, Penguin Classics and Arkana – and how to order them, write to us at the appropriate address below. Please note that for copyright reasons the selection of books varies from country to country.

In the United Kingdom: Please write to *Dept JC, Penguin Books Ltd, FREEPOST, West Drayton, Middlesex, UB7 0BR.*

If you have any difficulty in obtaining a title, please send your order with the correct money, plus ten per cent for postage and packaging, to *PO Box No 11, West Drayton, Middlesex*

In the United States: Please write to *Dept BA, Penguin, 299 Murray Hill Parkway, East Rutherford, New Jersey 07073*

In Canada: Please write to *Penguin Books Canada Ltd, 2801 John Street, Markham, Ontario L3R 1B4*

In Australia: Please write to the *Marketing Department, Penguin Books Australia Ltd, P.O. Box 257, Ringwood, Victoria 3134*

In New Zealand: Please write to the *Marketing Department, Penguin Books (NZ) Ltd, Private Bag, Takapuna, Auckland 9*

In India: Please write to *Penguin Overseas Ltd, 706 Eros Apartments, 56 Nehru Place, New Delhi, 110019*

In the Netherlands: Please write to *Penguin Books Netherlands B.V., Postbus 3507, NL–1001 AH, Amsterdam*

In West Germany: Please write to *Penguin Books Ltd, Friedrichstrasse 10–12, D–6000 Frankfurt/Main 1*

In Spain: Please write to *Alhambra Longman S.A., Fernandez de la Hoz 9, E–28010 Madrid*

In Italy: Please write to *Penguin Italia s.r.l., Via Como 4, I-20096 Pioltello (Milano)*

In France: Please write to *Penguin France S.A., 17 rue Lejeune, F-31000 Toulouse*

In Japan: Please write to *Longman Penguin Japan Co Ltd, Yamaguchi Building, 2–12–9 Kanda Jimbocho, Chiyoda-Ku, Tokyo 101*